AF624437

RABINDRANATH TAGORE
AND
FIFTY YEARS
OF
SAHITYA AKADEMI

Biswajit Sinha

Eastern Book Linkers

Delhi : : (India)

Publishers :
EASTERN BOOK LINKERS
5825, New Chandrawal, Jawahar Nagar,
Delhi-110007
Ph. : 23850287, 32919869
e-mail : ebl@vsnl.net

© Author

First Edition : 2006

Price : 300.00

ISBN : 81-7854-107-6

Printed at : **R.K. Print Service, Delhi**

PREFATORY

This book is my tribute to Rabindranath Tagore on the ensuing happy occasion of the Golden Jubilee Celebration of the Sahitya Akademi, the National Academy of Letters. The highest honour conferred by the Akademi on a writer is by electing him as its Fellow. This honour is reserved for 'The immortals of literature' and my present endeavour here is to honour 'The perennial inspirer of its Fellows', none other than Rabindranath. In this slim volume, I have tried to document how Sahitya Akademi, the highest literary organisation of this country has from time to time rekindled our interest in this master of Indian literature. Gurudeva was nor just a creative genius, but a man of deep human understanding, a social thinker of great compassion. A seer of the east, Rabindranath was eventually accepted worldwise as a universal man of profound vision. This monograph reconnoitre only those activities of the Sahitya Akademi that revolves around this great humanitarian artist.

Sahitya Akademi, the apex academy of literature in India came into being when the wounds of partition had not completely healed. At that time, it was a country with huge problems, centred mainly on poverty and mass illiteracy. This was one of the world's poorest and least developed nations. India was passing through acute economic hardships and put all its efforts and endeavours for industrial growths and advancements in the field of science and technology. That was also harsh times for it. But a country with long and glorious cultural past could not ignore its artistic legacies. It had learnt a lesson from its two centuries heinous history and was infact looking for cultural unity through the medium of arts and literature. Keeping this in mind, the Government of India established three distinct National Akademies for Visual, Performing and Literary Arts, all located in New Delhi. In the domain of literature, came up Sahitya Akademi, the National Akademi of Letters. "*Indian Literature is one though written in many languages*" became the slogan of the Sahitya Akademi and soon it acquired a pre-eminent place in the National set up as one of the Cultural forces in the process of binding the nation. It has embraced languages more than the recognised languages in India. It accepts that each has produced a literature of great vitality and richness. Though distinctive in parts all stand for a homogenous culture that is the essence of great Indian literature.

Next year this National Centre for Literature will be celebrating its Golden Jubilee and this perhaps pleasantly ironic that when the celebration is approaching, to quote Prof. K. Satchidanandan, "the news is around of many deaths : the deaths of the printed word, the death of Indian languages, the death of literatures of the regions, the death of rural cultures, of folk forms, of the tribal lore, when even the death of freedom of expression in the country. Sahitya Akademi. I am happy to say, is fruitfully engaged in the act of retrieval, the retrieval of cultural memory from fatal amnesia, of Indian languages and literatures from potential death, of our specific cultural identities from the forced standardisation and Westernization that globalisation seeks. We uphold the freedom of the writer and the artist to express themselves imaginatively and oppose all the obscurantist forces striving to crush that freedom. We defend the diversity of Indian culture and literature that is the source of its variety and richness, without at the sometime, historical, philosophical and aesthetic links that keep them

Ramkinkar Baij

(Renowned sculptor whose 'bust of Tegore' is installed at the Rabindra Bhavan)

united in a continuous dialogues among themselves and between the regional and the national, or the desi and the margi manifestations of Indian culture....." But one should not gloss over the fact that there will always be mixed feelings when the role of the present day writers or the literary institutions will be debate. Are today's younger generation of writers truly working as the cultural workers of this country of leading literary institutions truly exploring valid issues and the problems and solutions? The writers should not write just for aesthetic pleasure and similarly literary organisation owe a sacred duty to society not only to keep up the vitality of literature, but also raise questions concerning humanity that inspires its pious clientele to write.

It is quite natural for Sri Shafi Saida, a Sahitya Akademi laureate to express his deep anguish over the current trend of violence in the country. He compares India to a person lying bleeding and injured from head to toe. Today every individual of this country is expressing his or her grave concern at the communal and other disturbance in the country. Older writer veteran Vishu Prabhakar stresses upon the need of the writers community to use their pen as a useful weapon to counteract the evil forces working in society. The writer is for the society and has a responsibility towards it as well. The country is passing through harsh times and the writers community and above all, literary organisations must come forward to encounter them.

A writer ought to be a humanist. Here I am reminded of Tagore. The living older writers, the middle generation writers and the young writers, all thc three levels of writers must agree with me that as humanist, Rabindranath Tagore surpasses all. Nemai Sadhan Bose writes "though Rabindranath had dissociated himself from active politics, he continued to take interest in the freedom movement... in its struggle, not only against British imperialism, but also against socio-economic oppression, inequality, grinding poverty and backwardness." Through his writings, Rabindranath stood for the good of the world and in return, the whole world accoladed this great litterateur with the much coveted Nobel Prize for his literary excellence, but soon he proved that he is equally gifted in intellectual and philosophical exercises. Gurudeva, the seer of the east, went on to connect the whole world to become a universal man. After the historic incident of 1913 Rabindranath became an example and ideal of the ultimate that an Indian poet could aspire for : "Infact for the first time this master litterateur from Asia drew the attention of the world to the India's literary potentials. Till then, the West knew only about our classical literatures." This historic event occurred in colonial situation and few years later India won her battle against the British regime. But by that time Tagore was no more with us. But how could his country men forget the person who brought world wide fame to his motherland, when the latter was shackled in chains. He came to be known not only as a great writer but also as an able spokesman of modern India, whose creativity and thought is for *visva sreyas,* for the good of the world. Thus, in the post-independence phase, when the three leading cultural centres sprang up, it was decided to house them in one building and be named "Rabindra Bhavan" whose versatile genius encompassed the activities of all the three Akademies. He was a writer, dramatist, musician, a painter and so on. And a bust of Tagore, made by renowned sculptor Ramkinkar Baij was also installed. What a befitting tribute! Needless to mention about those innumerable societies, research centres, cultural forums, educational institutions, literary bodies than followed, all named after this great soul.

CONTENTS

Prefatory *iii*

1. Inauguration of Sahitya Akademi 11
2. Akademi Offices and Rabindra Bhavan 14
3. Tagore Centenary Celegration 18
4. Birth Anniversary of Tagore 46
5. Tagore Seminars, Workshops and Literary Forums 54
6. Exhibitions on Tagore 103
7. Tagore Translators : Akademi Laureates 126
8. Tagore Publications 132
9. Samvatsar Lectures 144

1

INAUGURATION OF SAHITYA AKADEMI

In the year 1994, the Government of India accepted in principle, the proposal of the then Royal Asiatic Society of Bengal to set up a National Cultural Trust. It stated that the Trust should be set up to encourage activities in all domains. It would embody three Akademies—one in Letters, one in Visual arts and one for Dance, Drama and Music. From the speech of Maulana Abul Kalam Azad. Minister for Education, at the inaugural meeting of Sahitya Akademi, we come to know that after the National Government was established in 1947, three conferences were convened to workout in detail the implications of this proposal. The conferences agreed about the need for the Akademies but felt that since a National Government had now been established, it was not necessary to set up a National Trust. Steps should however, be taken to set up the Akademies as autonomous bodies and provide them with the funds necessary for the work. The Government of India accepted that recommendation, but at the outset, made its position clear that it would act mainly as curtainraiser. Once the Akademies are founded, the Government would refrain from exercising any control and leave the Akademies to perform their functions as autonomous institutions.

The Sahitya Akademi was established under a Government of India Resolution dated 15 December 1952 in which the constitution of the Akademi was originally embodied. Described it as a national organisation to work actively for the development of Indian letters and to set high literary standards, to foster and co-ordinate literary activities in all the Indian languages and to promote through them all the cultural unity of the country. The Government of India formally inaugurated the Sahitya Akademi only on 12 March 1954, in the Central Hall of Parliament, New Delhi. The proceedings were inaugurated by Maulana Abul Kalam Azad who explained the aims, objectives and need for such an apex institutions Dr. Radha Krishnan, the Vice-Chairman of the Akademi informed the gathering that "The phrase, *Sahitya Akademi,* combines two words : '*Sahitya*' is Sanskrit, and '*Akademi*' is Greek. This name suggests our universal outlook and aspiration. Sahitya is a literary composition; Akademi is an assembly of men who are interested in the subject. So Sahitya Akademi will be an assembly of all those who are interested in creative and critical literature. It is the purpose of this Akademi to recognise men of achievement in letters, to encourage men of promise in letters, to educate public taste and to improve standards of literature and literary criticism. These are the aims which the Akademi has set to itself." Thus, the Sahitya Akademi came into being. I feel it necessary to mention here that in the Akademi's history, the first man to quote Tagore was the then Minister for Education, Maulana Abul Kalam Azad who while speaking in the context of Sahitya Akademi's representation of Indian Language (It incorporated all the 14 languages named in the Indian Constitution), stated in course of his inaugural address"... Tagore, who is the greatest poet of modern India, had been writing in Bengali ever since his childhood but his fame was not fully recognised even in his own province till the English version of Gitanjali declared him as one of the greatest poets of the world." This statement was recorded by Dr. S. Radhakrishnan, the first Vice-Chairman of Sahitya

Akademi, Whom I quote here "The intellectual renaissance through which we are passing is due to the impact of Western culture on Indian society and thought and this impact came to us through the medium of the English language. Many of these writers who are responsible for this renaissance– I need not mention the names, several names have already been mentioned : Gandhiji, Tagore, Sri Aurobindo, our Chairman Nehru himself-are responsible for bringing about an altogether new orientation of ideas and outlook in our country. It is therefore only proper that this Akademi should recognise English also as a language to be taken into account." This was in the morning of 12th March 1954, a historic event in the history of Indian literature.

2

AKADEMI OFFICES AND RABINDRA BHAVAN

Though Sahitya Akademi was founded in the year 1954, but it had no habitation and looking for a suitable office accommodation. It started with a provisional office accommodation in one of the rooms in the Ministry of Education. The next year, its Secretariat moved to the Theatre Communication Building, small rooms in hutments in Connaught Place, New Delhi. There was Akademi offices, library and reading room in the building. The building is long demolished with other offices of the time where once stood Bharat Sevak Samaja, post office and an open air coffee house etc. etc.

Today with the vicissitude of time, on this site, one can find a huge under-ground market complex now known to everyone as' Palika Bazar".

In 1955, the Ministry of Education agreed to provide funds for the construction of a common building for all three Akademies. The Ministry of Works, Housing and Supply had kindly allotted a three-acre plot for the purpose at the junction of the Janpath and Queen Victoria Road. The plans for the building were under preparation by the Central P.W.D. At that time there were certain temporary structure on the site reserved for the building. It was hoped that these structures would soon be removed and the vacant, possession of the plot made available to enable the foundation stone of the new building to be laid. The plans

Rabindra Bhavan, where the Sahitya Akademi is housed; designed by Sri H. Rehman and built by the Government of India for the three National Academies.

of the building was being jointly sponsored by the three Akademies. The building was expected to be a four storeyed one, the ground floor with the auditorium and other amenities for the common use of the Akademies and one floor each for the Akademies. But due to some administrative hurdles, site for the building had to be changed. Eventually in 1956, a 3-1/2 acre plot of land at the junction of the Ferozeshah and Lytton Roads was reserved by the Government of India for a common building for all the three National Akademies. By this time, the plans for the building was also finalised. However, it was not yet known as to when the actual construction would begin, as the final decision in the matters was to be taken by the Ministries of Education and Finance and depended on the availability of funds. But it was hoped that actual construction of the building would begin in 1959. The Government of Indian made generous grant and the three national Akademies was soon to have a building of their own, the foundation stone of which was laid by the President of India, Dr. Rajendra Prasad on 24 April 1959 and the Exhibition Hall was expected to be ready for formal inauguration in May 1961. The building was designed by Sri H. Rehman, Senior Architect of the Govt. of India. It was planned that along with main Secretariat block which would composed of three wings, one for each Akademi, there would be an auditorium and stage for experimental theatre and an Exhibition Hall.

Ultimately this took the form of a Y shaped elegant building, constructed by the C.P.W.D. with a generous grant made by the Govt. of India. In the Ministry of Scientific Research and Cultural Affairs. Adjacent to the main building is an Exhibition Hall which was formally inaugurated by the President of India to commemorate the Birth Centenary of Rabindranath Tagore on 8th May 1961, alongwith an exhibition of Tagore's life and works. On 11th Nov. 1961, the central office of the Sahitya Akademi shifted to this new premises in the newly constructed building at the junction of Ferozeshah and Lytton (now Copernicus) Roads. Building was named 'Rabindra Bhavan', from where run the Head office of the three Akademies. Thus the building was appropriately named in memory of one whose manifold creative genius was consistently dedicated to the service of his people and the cause of international understanding. Perhaps, the best homage to great son of India.

3
TAGORE CENTENARY CELEBRATION

In the very first year of its existence (1954-55), the Sahitya Akademi, to commemorate Tagore' Centenary declared, "It is fitting that this occasion should be celebrated on a national level and, if possible, international scale and should be well planned in advance". It further stated that 'Tagore belonged to the whole country and his centenary should be celebrated not in one place but in many places all over India and not by one organisation but by many. The celebrations may be of two kinds, one which embodies the nation's homage in some useful, concrete and lasting achievement, the other which is organised only for the occasion to express the people's grateful remembrance of one who added so richly to India's cultural heritage.

Under the first category may be included such items as a centenary edition of Tagore's collected works in Bengali (which may be published by Visva-Bharati), a selection of his writings to be translated and published in all major Indian languages and English, a good biography to be written by a competent writer, publication of an album of his paintings, institution of Tagore Chairs of Literature in some Indian Universities, etc. etc. Under the second category may be included such items as a literary conference, national or international Drama festivals. Exhibitions of Tagore's paintings and manuscripts, etc. etc."

These were just tentative suggestions. Letter were addressed to the State Governments. Universities, literary and cultural institutions as well as select individuals all over the country inviting their suggestions, hundreds of suggestions were received, sorted out and tabulated.

It was decided that the General council or the Executive Board would appoint an all India Committee to consider those suggestions and recommend a comprehensive and co-ordinated plan for the consideration of the Sahitya Akademi and the Government of India. Subsequently in the years 1956-57, an All-India Tagore Centenary Committee was set up to formulate and plan a comprehensive programme to celebrate in a fitting manner the 100th birth anniversary of Rabindranath Tagore due in 1961. Eight distinguished members of the Committee were

1. Sri Jawaharlal Nehru (Chairman)
2. Dr. S. Radhakrishnan
3. Dr. B.V. Keskar
4. Prof. Humayun Kabir
5. Dr. Satyendranath Bose (representing Visva-Bharati University).
6. Sri K.G. Saiyidain (representing the Ministry of Education).
7. Sri D.M. Sen (representing the West Bengal Govt.)
8. Sri Bimal Chandra Sinha (representing Rabindra Bharati, Calcutta.)

Now this centenary Committee was likely to meet in the early part of 1958 and digest of the suggestions received was to be placed before it. In the meanwhile, the Sahitya Akademi, in consultation with its Advisory Board for Bengali, planned a comprehensive selection of Tagore's Bengali works in eight volumes covering poems, songs, dramas, short stories, novels, essays and letters. These volumes were under translations in all the major Indian languages. Besides these, there was to be a special edition of the original Bengali text in Devanagari script.

On the invitation of the International Council for Philosophy and Humanistic Studies. Secretary of the Akademi was deputed to attend a meeting of the Expert Committee to advice UNESCO on the translation of Oriental Classics into western language. The meetings were held in Paris on 27th, 28 and 29th November 1957. The secretary was also deputed by the Ministry of Education to attend at the same time meeting of the executive Board of UNESCO. During this visit to Paris, the Secretary discussed the Centenary programme with the UNESCO authorities who agreed to consider UNESCO's active participation in the international aspects of the proposed celebrations. A detailed note was submitted to UNESCO in this connection.

Accordingly in March 1958, the All India Tagore Centenary Committee met to review the various suggestions received for celebration of the Tagores's Birth Centenary. The Committee approved the tentative outline of a comprehensive programme to be implemented during the centenary year in cooperation with the various agencies and institutions interested in the celebrations. The general outline of the programme was also approved since by the Government of India which invited the State Governments to sponsor the formations of non-Official Centenary Committees for each State which were to consider in detail the specific programme suitable for the region concerned and to help in its proper implementation.

The Ministry of Information and Broadcasting agreed to sponsor the production of a documentary of Tagore to be directed by the eminent film director, Sri Satyajit Ray. The All India Radio also planned a comprehensive programme on the air for the Jayanti year which included Hindi versions of some Tagore's famous musical plays or dance-dramas. The AIR also cooperated with the Sahitya Akademi in the preparation of Hindi renderings of select songs of Tagore, to be rendered in such a way to preserve the original tunes.

So far as Sahitya Akademi's share in this programme is concerned, action had already been taken. As stated earlier, by 1957-58, the first volume of the Devanagari edition (Ekottarsati-101 select poems with glossary) was published and the second volumes of 500 songs was in press. The Gujarat edition of select short stories was published. The Marathi version of the short stories by Mama Warerkar was ready for press. Translations in several Indian languages were under way. An Editorial Committee was setup to plan and edit a Tagore Centenary Volume. This high-power All India Tagore Centenary Committee had Prime Minister Sri Jawahar Lal Nehru as Chairman, the Vice-president of India. Dr. S. Radhakrishnan as Vice-Chairman, the Minister for culture. Prof. Humayun Kabir as Secretary and the Minister of Finance. Sri Gopala Reddi at the Treasurer.

During the years 1958-59, it was decided that alongwith Tagore Centenary Volume in English, there may be published in some Indian language similar centenary volumes containing contributions by distinguished writers in the languages concerned.

As said earlier, under the publication programme of first category, i.e. one giving the original Bengali text in Devanagari script, the third volume of 21 short stories was ready for press.

In the second series, the Gujarati translation of 21 short stories was already published, the Marathi and Punjabi editions were also printed for release; the Assamese edition of 101 poems was in press; the other volumes in the various languages were under preparation.

The Sahitya Akademi also started assisting in the compilation of select writings of Tagore in English to be brought out by Macmillan & Co. New York on the occasion of the Centenary. The volume was sponsored by the Hazen Foundation of New Haven and the Asia Society of New York; to be edited by Prof. Amiya Chakrabarty, an associate of Rabindranath Tagore. It was also desired that a similar volume be published in India.

The Rockefeller Foundation of the United States agreed to offer a travel-grant to the Secretary of the Sahitya Akademi to visit select foreign countries of his choice in order to further Sahitya Akademi's contacts with literary institutions and individuals in these countries. The invitation of the Rockefeller Foundation was placed before the Executive Board of the Sahitya Akademi. The Executive Board permitted the Secretary to accept the travel grant which was for a period of six months. The Secretary left Delhi on the 30th March 1959 and covered in his tour some twenty-two countries including South East Asia, Japan, the U.S.A. and Europe.

The Secretary discussed with institutions and individuals in the various countries interested in the life and work of Tagore, the plans and programmes envisaged by them for the centenary of the poet's birthday following next year. The Secretary returned to India on the 29th September 1959. Relevant information regarding those proposed plans and the names of the institutions interested in the centenary was sent by the Secretary to the All India Tagore Centenary Committee and the Visva-Bharati Shantiniketan. A note embodying this information was also to be sent to UNESCO in Paris. The interest shown by this international organisation in the Tagore Centenary was warmly welcomed. In the year 1959-60 it was declared that the Akademi would shortly bring out a slim volume on Tagore's life for children to be called *Kavi Katha* in various Indian languages. This short biography written in very lucid language will be priced low so as to be within the reach of young readers.

A small centenary volume in Urdu was also under preparation. The Akademi started helping some State Centenary Committees in the preparation of similar volumes in some other Indian languages. As mentioned earlier, the Akademi planned the publication of a centenary series of his select writings under the following heads (1) 101 poems; (2) 500 songs; (3) Twenty one short stories; (4) Seven Dramas; Visarjan, Chitrangada, Chirakumar Sabha, Raja, Dakghar, Mukhtadhara and Raktakarabi; (5) Three novels; Gora, Chokher Bali and Jogajog (6) Essays, religious, philosophic educational. social and political : (7) other prose writings including essays on literary themes, belles letters, autobiographical writing, travelogue and letters; (8) writings specially suitable for children.

These volumes now actually been started publishing in two series. In the first series it. included the original Bengali text in Devnagari Script. The first volume entitled Ekottarsati comprising of 101 poems was awarded a certificate of merit in the category of Book production in Indian language in the Fifth State Awards for excellence in printing and designing of books for 1959. The second volume titled *Gita-Panchasati* was already broughtout, containing 500 songs. The remaining volumes were in preparation.

In the second series, by this time, the following books were published : 21 Short stories of Tagore in Gujarati,

Marathi and Punjabi; the novels' Chokher Bali' in Marathi and Punjabi and 'Gora' in Punjabi.

Similarly, two volumes of select writings of Tagore in Nepali, two in Manipuri and one in Tibetan were under preparation. Thus it became clear that the Sahitya Akademies programme on the occasion of the Centenary of Tagore's Birth was chiefly concerned with making his writing better known. The Akademi published a Tagore Centenary Volume in English, a monumental compilation containing articles by renowned writers. Indian and foreign, on the various aspects of Tagore's life and works alongwith a Tagore chronicle and an useful bibliography of his works and few portraits of him by well known artists. The volume was formally released by the Vice-President, Dr. S. Radhakrishan on the 11th November 1961, on the occasion of the International Literary Seminar. (This is discussed in details under the head 'Akademi Publications'). Moreover it is necessary here to mention that a Tagore Homage volume under the title Ravindropaharam was also published in Malayalam. A small Centenary Volume in Urdu was under preparation. The Akademi helped some State Centenary Committees in the preparation of similar volumes in some other Indian languages. The Sahitya Akademi sponsored a new edition of the Tamil work entitled 'Rabindranath Tagore' by Sri K. Chandrasekharan. Another Significant worked titled 'A Tagore Reader' edited by Prof. Amiya Chakravarty was broughtout. This volume was sponsored by the Hazen Foundation of New Haven and the Asia Society of New York. This book that was published on the occasion included the select writings of Tagore in English and was published from New York by Macmillan and Co.. By this time, the Devanagari editions of 101 poems, 500 songs and of the novel 'Chokher Bali' published. In translation projects, 101 poems in Malayalam and Tamil; 21 short stories in

Gujarati, Hindi, Malayalam, Marathi, Oriya, Punjabi and Tamil got published; also appeared select plays in Kannada, Marathi (vol., II) and Tamil, 'Chokher Bali' in Hindi, Marathi, Punjabi and Telugu; Gora in Hindi, Punjabi and Telugu. A volume of select poems in Tibetan also came out. For young readers, a Bengali text by Smt. Lila Majumdar entitled 'Kavi Katha', a short biographical sketch was broughtout and it got translated into all major language of India such as Assamese, Gujarati, Hindi, Kannada, Kashmiri, Malayalam, Sindhi, Tamil, Telugu, Urdu and also English version.

After several years of planning and elaborate preparations, finally it was decided in 1959 that as part of the Centenary programme during the Tagore week in November 1961 the Sahitya Akademi would conduct on **International Literary Seminar** in New Delhi, under the joint auspices of the Sahitya Akademi and the Indian Council for Cultural Relations In consultation with the Vice-President and the Minister of Scientific Research and Cultural Affairs, the plan of the seminars was drawn up and was finally approved by the President of the Akademi. It was decided that about twenty foreign delegates and fifty Indian delegates would be invited to participate in the seminar that would discuss three themes :

1. *Rabindranath Tagore and Modern Indian Literature.*
2. *Impact of Tagore on the West.*
3. *Literature and Modern Life.*

UNESCO declared that it would offer a grant of ten thousand dollars to meet the travel expenses of foreign delegates. International Literary Seminar was inaugurated by Dr. S. Radhakrishan, Vice-President of India, on November 11, 1961, marked the first major event of the Tagore week in Delhi which was inaugurated simultaneously.

The seminar lasted for three days, 12, 13 and 14 November, and discussed the following three themes :

1. *Rabindranath Tagore and modern Indian Literature.*
2. *Rabindranath Tagore and the world.*
3. *Literature and Modern Life.*

25 distinguished writers from 16 countries and 39 representing 16 languages of India took part in this four day International Seminar, held at Vigyan Bhavan, New Delhi (Detailed Information appears in the following chapter under the heading "Tagore Seminars".

A special event of the Tagore Centenary, Celebration was the announcement of a special; **'Tagore Awards'** of Rs. 10,000/- to a living Indian author whose studies, writing or editings had helped most in the understanding of Tagore life and ideas. The Executive Board of the Sahitya Akademi, set up a Special Committee to declare the Award on the basis of confidential recommendation invited from the members of the various Advisory Boards of the Akademi. The Committee deemed four writers as equally deserving of the Award and recommended that the amount set apart for the award be divided equally among them. The prestigious Award was given by the Vice-President, Dr. S. Radhakrishnan on the occasion of the inauguration of the International Literary Seminar to the recipients : Shri Prabhat Kumar-Mukhopadhyay (Bengali); Sri Pulinbihari Sen (Bengali); Dr. Hazariprasad Dwivedi (Hindi) and Sri Akurati Chalmayya (Telugu).

Laureate Prabhat Kumar Mukhopadhyay was born on 27 July, 1892 at Ranaghat in Nadia district of West Bengal. He came to Shantiniketan at the age of 17 and lived there even since. He was Librarian of Visva-Bharati Library, Shantiniketan from 1918-1954. He had to his credits a number of scholarly works. Bharate jatiya andolan, (a history of Nationalist movement in India) (1925) Banga Parichay, 2 vols. (1936-1942) Jnana-bharati, geographical dictionary in two volumes, 1940-41; a comprehensive four volumes biography of Rabindranath Tagore in Bengali titled *Rabindra Jibani*, (1946-1956) to name a few.

The second Awardee Pulinbahri Sen was born in 1908. He will be remembered for his compilation and editing a number of Tagore's works and also Tagore bibliographies. He was the editor of Bangiya Sahitya Parishad Patrika and edited the Abanindranath Tagore Number of the Journal of the Indian Society of Oriental Art. He also edited a collection of poems of Pramatha Chaudhuri. His 'Patrabali' is a collection of letters from J.C. Bose to Rabindranath Tagore. His book 'Rabindrayan', in two volumes was well received.

Another winner of the Tagore Prize was Dr. Hazari Prasad Dwivedi, one of the front ranking writers in Hindi. He was born in 1907 in village Dubeka Chapra of district Ballia in U.P. Educated in the Sanskrit, tradition of the family, he received the degree of Jyotishacharya from Banaras Hindi University in 1930. Dwivedi took his teaching job in Shantiniketan and served as the Director of Hindi Bhavan from 1940 to 1950. He became the Head of the Hindi Department at Banaras Hindu University in 1950. In 1960 he joined the Punjab University as its head in Hindi Department. He became the Chairman of the U.P. Hindi Granth Akademi. Hazari Prasad Dwivedi was attached to a number of literary institutions. He was the President of Hindi Sahitya Sammelan in 1946. He was one of the founding member of the Sahitya Akademi, a member of its Execurtive Board. Dwivedi was also a member of the first official language commission. In 1957, this scholar was awarded Padmabhushan. Besides this special Tagore Centenary Award of 1961, the same Sahitya Akademi selected his book 'Alok Parva' a collection of twenty seven essays as the best book in Hindi and conferred on him Sahitya Akademi Award' of 1973 in the language. Some of his notable publications are *Sura Sahitya* (criticism) 1936; *Hindi Sahitya Ki Bhumika* (literary history) 1940; Kabir (criticism) 1942; *Banabhatta Ki Atmakatha* (novel) 1946; *Ashoke ke phul* (essay); 1948; *Madhya Kalin Dharma Sadhana* (religion); 1952, *Hindi Sahitya* 1952. *Nath Siddhon Ki Baniyan* (ed. 1957). *Meghdut : Ek Purani Kahani* (1957); *Vichar-pravaha* (essays 1959), *Charuchadralekh* (novel, 1963). *Punarnava* (novel, 1973) and *Anandas Ka Potha* (novel, 1976). This renowned scholar died in 1979.

The last recipient of Tagore Award was Akurati Chalamayya who was born on 12 January 1903 in Epurpalem of District Guntur in Andhra Pradesh. He received his education in Visva-Bharati and published a sizeable number of books and was an astute translator. His noteworthy publications are *Visvakavi Rabindruni Jivitamu Sandesamu* (life and message), appeared in 1946, *Gandhiji Charitrau-panyasamulu* (life and lectures) published in 1951; *Netaji Bose Babu Charitra-upanyasamulu* (life and lectures), appeared in 1952. *Akurtichalamayya* rendered *Shantiniketan*, *Vidya* and *Gora*, all from Tagore.

As discussed eariler, the International Literary Seminar was organised by the Sahitya Akademi and the Indian Council for Cultural Relations, with the assistance of UNESCO, as part of the Tagore Centenary celebrations in India. Its inauguration marked the first major event of the Tagore Week in Delhi which was inagurated simultaneously.

The programme of the Seminar, of which the inaugural and the concluding sessions were open to the public (by invitation) is given below. A limited number of Observers had been invited to attend the closed sessions of the Seminar on the 12th, 13th and 14th November.

Programme

Inauguration of Tagore Week and Opening of International Literary Seminar

Saturday, 11 November, 1961

Venu	:	Vigyan Bhavan, Main Hall
3.15 p.m.		Rabindra Sangeet
3.20 p.m.		Welcome Speech by Sri Humayun Kabir, Minister, Scientific Research & Cultural Affairs.
3.35 p.m.		Presentation of Rabindra-Puraskar (Tagore Award) by Dr. S. Radhakrishnan, Vice-President of India.
3.45 p.m.		Inaugural Address by the Vice-President of India.
4.05 p.m.		Speeches and messages by some foreign delegates.
4.30 p.m.		Vote of thanks by Sri B. Gopala Reddi, Minister, Works, Housing & Supply, and Treasurer, Rabindranath Tagore Centenary Committee.
4.35 p.m.		Rabindra Sangeet
5.00 p.m.		Reception by the Minister, Scientific Research and Cultural Affairs, at Rashtrapati Bhavan

Seminar Sessions

Sunday, 12 November, 1961

10.00 a.m. to 1.00 p.m.

Venue	:	Committee Room B. Vigyan Bhavan
Chairman	:	Sri Humayun Kabir

Subject : Rabindranath Tagore and Modern Indian Literature

Speakers : Sanskrit—Dr. Suniti Kumar Chatterjee

Telugu—Sri B. Gopala Reddi

Assamese—Dr. Birinchi Kumar Barua

Bengali—Dr. Sukumar Sen

Discussion

11.30 a.m. Ten-minute interval for coffee

Gujarati—Sri Kakasaheb Kalelkar

English—Dr. Mulk Raj Anand

Hindi—Dr. Hazariprasad Dwivedi

Kannada—Prof. V.K. Gokak

Discussion

1.15 p.m. Lunch by the Vice-President of India at Rashtrapati Bhavan

Sunday, 12 November, 1961

3 p.m. to 5.30 p.m.

Venue : Committee Room B. Vigyan Bhavan

Chairman : Sri Humayun Kabir

Subject : Rabindranath Tagore and Modern Indian Literature

Speakers : Kashmiri—Sri J.L. Kaul

Malayalam—Sri G. Sankara Kurup

Marathi—Smt. Kusumavati Deshpande

Oriya—Sri Kalindi Charan Panigrahi

Discussion

4.15 p.m. Ten-minute interval for coffee

Punjabi—Sri Balwant Gargi

Sindhi—Prof. L.H. Ajwani

Tamil—Sri K. Chandrasekharan

Urdu—Dr. Masud Husain Khan

Discussion

Chairman's concluding remarks

Monday, 13 November, 1961

10 a.m. to 1.00 p.m.

Venue : Committee Room B. Vigyan Bhavan

Chairman : Sri Humayun Kabir

Subject : Rabindranath Tagore and the World

Speakers : Sir Isaiah Berlin (United Kingdom)

Dr. Zaki Naguib Mahmoud (U.A.R.)

Prof. Giuseppe Tucci (Italy)

Dr. H.S. Nyberg (Sweden)

Dr. Clovis Maksoud (League of Arab States) Discussion

11.30 a.m. Ten-minute interval for coffee

Speakers : Mr. Louis Untermeyer (U.S.A.)

Prince Prem Purachatra (Thailand)

Dr. Dusan Zbavitel (Czechoslovakla)

Mr. Martin Wickremsinghe (Ceylon)

Chairman's concluding remarks

1.15 p.m. Lunch by Minister, Scientific Research and Cultural Affairs, at Hyderabad House

Monday, 13 November, 1961

3 p.m. to 5.30 p.m.

Venue : Committee Room B. Vigyan Bhavan

Chairman : Sri Humayun Kabir

Subject : Literature and Modern Life

Speakers : Mr. Aldous Huxley

Mr. Vsevolod Ivonov (U.S.S.R.)

Discussion

4.15 p.m. Ten-minute interval for coffee

Speakers : Dr. Zaki Naguib Mahmoud (U.A.R.)

Discussion

Tuesday, 14 November, 1961

10 a.m. to 1.00 p.m.

Venue : Committee Room B. Vigyan Bhavan

Chairman : Sri Humayun Kabir

Subject : Literature and Modern Life

Speaker : Mr. Louis Untermeyer (U.S.A.) Discussion

11.30 a..n. Ten-minute interval for coffee

Mr. Hans Erich Nossack (West Germany)

Discussion

Concluding Session (open to public by invitation)

Tuesday, 14 November, 1961

3.15 p.m.

Venue : Main Hall, Vigyan Bhavan

Chairman : Dr. S. Radhakrishnan

Rabindra-Sangeet

Speeches by some deligetates

Chairman's concluding remarks

Vote of thanks

Rabindra-Sangeet

Wednesday, 15 November, 1961, and Thursday, 16 November, 1961 :

Sight-seeing in Delhi, including visitis to places of historical interest, the National Museum, Tagore Exhibition, etc.

FOREGIN DELEGATES

Berlin, Isaiah (Sir) (b. 1909)

Chichele Professor of Social and Political Theory, Oxford, since 1957, Visiting Lecturer, Harvard University, 1949, 1951, 1953 : Alexander White professor, Chicago University, 1955. Publications : *Karl Marx,* 1939; *The Inevitability of History,* 1954; *The Age of Enlightement,* 1956 : etc.

Chelyshev, E.P.

Soviet Linguist and critic. Director of the Foreign Languages Institute, Moscow University.

Guehenne, Jean (b. 1890)

French essayist and literary critic : Inspector General of the Universities ; Publications : Biography of Rousseau, *Caliban Parle,* 1928 ; *Conversion A L'Humain,* 1931; *Jeunesse De La France,* 1936; and several Diarlies.

Hagelstange Rudolf

German poet, essayist and novelist; Member, German Academy for Language and Literature, the Bavarian Academy of Fine Arts and the German P.E.N. centre : Awarded German Critics Prize in 1952 and the Distinction of the German Schiller Foundation in 1955. Publications : *Storm Der Zeit* (Stream of Time. poems) : *Offen Gesagt* (Speaking Frankly, essays); etc.

Huxley, Aldous

British author, at present resident in the U.S.A. Publications : *Crome Yellow,* 1921; Antic Hay, 1923, *Jesting Pilate,* 1926; *Point Counter point,* 1928; *Brave New World,* 1932; Eyeless in Gaza, 1936; *Ends and Means,* 1937; *Time Must Have a Stop,* 1944; *The Perennial Philosophy,* 1946; *Ape and Essence,* 1948; etc.

Ivonov, Vsevolod Vyacheslavovich

Soviet novelist and short-story writer, Published his first story in 1915 which attracted the attention of Gorki. Publications : Colored Winds, 1922; *Mystery of Mysteries,* 1927; *Adventures of a Fakir,* 1934-35 (all novels;) etc.

Khashab, Yehya A L

Director of the Cultural Department of the League of Arab States.

Kora, Tomiko (Madame)

Social worker and member of Japanese Parliament; was closely associated with Tagore during his visits to Japan.

Mahmoud, Zaki Naguib

Professor of philosophy, Cairo University. Visiting lecurer in U.S.A. 1953-54; Editor-in-Chief, *Al-Thaquafa;* Publications; *History of World Literature,* 4 vols. (1942-1947); *Positivistic Logic,* 1931; *On Scientific Philosophy,* 1958; (in English) *Self Determination,* 19447; *The Land and the People of Egypt,* 1958; etc.

Maksoud Clovis

Representative of the League of Arab National, New Delhi.

Matsuoka Yoko (Madame)

Secretary-General, International P.E.N., Tokyo, Japan.

Nossack, Hans Erich

Poet, novelist and essayist from West Germany, Member; Academy of Arts, Hamburg : Academy for Language and Poetry, Darmstadt; Publications : *Spirale* (novel) and *Die Hauptprobe* (play); etc.

Nyberg, H.S.

Swedish Academician and Orientalist; Professor of Semitic Languages in Uppsala (1931-56); Member of the Swedish Academy of Literature, History and Antiquities; of the Academy of Sciences, Stockholm; Honorary member of the Royal Asiatic Society, London; of the Societe Asiatique, Paris; of the German Oriental Society; Author of several works on Arabic and Islamic subjects and on the Old Testament. Publications include *Hilfsbuch des Pehlevi,* 2 vols., 1928-31; *Die Religionen Des Alten Iran,* 1937; etc.

Purachatra, Prem (Prince)

Siamese educator, poet and play-wright, Head of the Department of Modern Languages, Chulalongkorn Universkty, 1942, Co-Chairman, UNESCO East-West Colloquium, Brussels, 1958; President of Thai P.E.N. Centre; Member of the Committee for Tagore Centenary Celebrations in Bangkok, 1961, Publications : Magic Lotus, (drama, 1937) : *Siamese Idyll,* (poetry, 1945); *The Story of Khun Chang Khun Phan,* (novel, 1955); etc.

Suratgar, Lutfli; Professor, University of Tehran, Iran.

Tucci, Giuseppe

Professor of Religions and Philosophy of India and the Far East at the University of Rome; President, ISMEO; Has made more than six voyags in Nepal and eight scientific expenditions to western and central Tibet; has directed, since 1956, archaeological campaigns in Pakistan, Afghanistan and Iran, Publications : *Shrines of a Thousand Buddhas,* 1936; *Tibetan Painted Scrolls,* 1949; *Minor Buddhist Texts,* 1956-58; etc.

Untermeyer, Louis

American author and editor; Consultant in Poetry, the Library of Congress, Washington D.C.; Publications: *Moses* (novel) 1928; *Heinrich Heine : Paradox and Poet,* (2 vols., 1937); *Modern American Poetry* (8th edition, 1951); *Modern British Poetry* (7th edition, 1951); *Walt Whitman,* 1949; etc.

Vidmar, Josep

President of Writers' Association of Yugoslavia; President of the Council of Nationalities of the Federal People's Assembly; President of the Presidium of People's Assembly of Slovania; Professor at the Academy of Dramatic Arts of Ljubijana; Member of the Academy of Sciences and Arts of Slovania. Publications : *Cultural Problems of Slavanianism, Literary Criticism; Meditations;* etc.

Wickresinghe, Martin

Ceylonese scholar and author; Publications; *Aspects of Sinhalese Culture, The Mysticism of Lowrence. The Buddhist Jataka Stories;* etc.

Zbavitel, Dusan

Czech Orientalist.

INDIAN DELEGATES

Ajwani, L.H. Sindh

Essayist and critic; Member Executive Board of Sahitya Akademi; Principal, National College, Bandra, Bombay; Publications; *Immortal India; Uchhal;* etc.

Anand, Mulk Raj

Novelist and art-critic; Editor 'Marga'; has published more than 30 books in English; *Untouchable,* 1935; *Coolie,* 1936; *Two Leaves and a Bud,* 1937 (all novels); *Persian Painting* (essays) 1938; etc.

Barua, Birinchi Kumar

Assamese critic and novelist; Member of Executive Board, Sahitya Akademi; Publications; *Ankia Nat,* critism, 1940; *Jibanar Batat,* novel *Assamese Literature,* 1944; etc.

Barua, Hem

Assamese poet and essayist; Member of Parliament; Publications; *Agastya Viplav aru Asam,* history, 1948; *Sanmihali,* 1957; *The Red River and the Blue Hill,* 1954; etc.

Barua, Navakant

Assamese poet and novelist; Publications: *He Aranya He Mahasagar,* poems, 1951; *Kapili Pariya Sadhu,* novel, 1955; etc.

Bendre, D.R.

Kannada poet and critic; Winner of Akademi Award;

Member, Executive Board of Sahitya Akademi; Publications; Gari, poems, 1930; *Sahitya Samsodhana,* criticism, 1941; *Aralu-Maralu,* poems, 1957.

Bhattacharya, Bhabani

Novelist and short-story writer in English, Publications; *The Golden Boat* (translation for Tagore); *So Many Hungers; Music for Mohini; He Who Rides a Tiger; A Goddess Named Gold;* (all novels). etc. Editor and Chief Translator of *Towards Universal Man* (Selected Essays of Tagore).

Chandrasekharan. K

Tamil essayist and historian of literature; Publications; *Sanskrit Literature;* An Approach to Indian Art; etc.

Chatterji, Suniti Kumar

Bengali linguist and orientalist; Padmabhushana; Khaira Professor of Linguistics and Phonetics. 1922-51; Visiting Professor in the University of Pennysylvania, 1951; Chairman of the West Bengal Legislative Council, 1956; Chairman, Government of India Sanskrit Commission: Publictions: *Origin and Development of the Bengali Language.* 2 vols., 1926; *Indo-Aryan and Hindi,* 1941; *Rajasthani-Bhasha; Bharater Bhasha a Bhasha Samasya, 1945;* etc.

Chettiar, A.C.

Tamil critic and essayist; Translator of Shakespeare's *Othello;* Professor of Tamil, Annamalai University; visited International Oriental Conference, Moscow, as a delegate of Indian Government.

Daulatram, Jairamdas

Member of Parliament; was Minister of Food and

Agriculture, Union Government and Governor of Bihar and Assam; Publications; *A Week with Gandhiji in Prison; Problems of the Frontier; The Ancestry of Sindhi;* etc.

Deshpande, Kusumavati (Smt.)

Marathi essayist and historian of literature; President, Marathi Sahitya Sammelan; Publications; *Dip-Kali,* 1934; *Dip Dan,* 1940; *Marathi Kadamabariche Pahile Shatak,* 2 vols., criticism, 1954; etc.

Dinkar, Ramdhari Sinha

Hindi poet, historian and essayist; Padmabhushana; Awarded prizes by the Government of India, Bihar Rashtra Bhasha Parishad and Sahityakar Samsad; Allahabad, for distinguished work in poetry; Winner of Akademi Award; Publications; *Renuka,* 1935; *Kurukshetra,* 1946 (poetry); *Samskriti Ke Char Adhyaya* (history), 1955; *Urvashi* (poetry). 1960; etc.

Dwivedi, Hazari Prasad

Hindi critic, essayist and novelist; Head of the Department of Hindi, Punjabi University, Chandigarh; Member, Executive Board of Sahitya Akademi; Publications: *Hindi Sahitya Ki Bhoomika,* literary history, 1940; *Kabir,* criticism, 1942; *Banbhatta Ki Atmakatha,* novel, 1946; *Ashok Ke Phul,* essays, 1948; Lal Kaner, translation of Tagore's play; etc.

Gargi, Balwant

Punjabi dramatist and critic. Publications: *Loha Kut,* 1944; *Kesro,* 1952; *Kanak di Balli,* 1954 (all plays); Folk Theatre in India, etc.

Gokak, V.K.

Kannada poet. novelist and critic; Director of Central

Institute of English, Hyderabad; Winner of Akademi Award; President. All India Karnatak Literary Conference, 1957; Delegate. Fifth Conference of Poets in Belgium, 1960 and International P.E.N. Conference, Tokyo, 1957; Publictions; *the Poetic Approach to Language,* criticism, 1952; *The Song of Life,* poems, 1948; etc.

Husain Ehtesham

Urdu critic and essayist; Reader, University of Allahabad; Member, Hindustani Academy (U.P.); has travelled in U.S.A. and England as Rockfeller Fellow 1952-53. Publications: *Virane, short stories, 1943;* Tanqidi Jaeze criticism 1944; *Zauk-e-Abad our Shaoor, criticism,* 1955; etc.

Jainendra Kumar

Hindi novelist, short-story writer and essayist; has published more than 23 books, *notably Parakh,* 1930; *Sunita,* 1936; *Tyagapatra,* 1937; *Jaivardhan,* 1958 (all novels).

Joshi, Umashankar

Gujarati poet and essayist : Editors. *Sanskriti;* Director of the University School of Gujarati language and literature, 1954; Member, Executive Board, Sahitya Akademi; Publications; *Vishvashanti,* 1931, *Gangotri, Nisheeth* (all poems); Sapna Bhara (one-act plays); *Shravani Melo* (short stories); etc.

Kalelkar, Kakasaheb

Member of Parliament; author of several works in Gujarati, Marathi and Hindi; closely associated with Gandhiji; Publications; Lokmata and *Jeevan Lila,* travelogues; and several translations of Tagore.

Kaul, J.L.

Kashmiri critic and essayist; Member, Executive Board of Sahitya Akademi; Publications; Kashmiri Literature, 1944; Interpretations of Ghalib, 1957; etc.

Khan, Masud Husain

Urdu poet, critic and lingulist; Reader, Department of Urdu, Aligarh University; visiting Associate Professor in University of California, Berkeley; Publications; Tarikh-i-Zaban-i-Urdu (History of Urdu language), *Do Neem* (poems); Hindi : *Roop Bengal* (poems); etc.

Kurup. G. Sankara

Malayalam poet and critic; has published fifteen volumes of poperty; translated Omar Khayyam's *Rubayat; Kalidsa's Meghaduta and* Tagore's *Gitanjali.*

Mansimha, Mayadhar

Oriya poet and historian of literature; Profesor of Oriya, Utkal University; Publications; *Dhuna, Akshyata, Karusa* (poems). *Buddha* (play); etc.

Mitra, Premendra

Bengali poet, short-story writer and novelist; Winner of Akademi Award; Publicatioins; *Prathama,* 1933; *Sagar Theke Phera* (poems) 1956; *Putul a Pratima* (short stories). 1934; etc.

Mohan Singh

Punjabi poet and essayist; Member, Executive Board of Sahitya Akademi; Winner of Akademi Award; Publications; *Save Pattar,* 1936; *Adhvate,* 1943; *Avazan,* 1954; *Vadda Vela* (all poems).

Mukherji, Prabhat Kumar

Bengali Historian and Biographer; closely asociated with Tagore and Santiniketan; Reciplent of 'Rabindra Memorial Prize', West Bengal Government, 1957; *Publications; Rabindra Jivani* (Tagore's Biography in 4 vols.); *Jnan Bharati* (Bengali Encyclopedia) 1940; etc.

Narayan. R.K.

Novelist and short-story writer in English; Winner of Akademi Award; Publications; *Swami and Friends,* 1935; *The Dark Room,* 1938; *Waiting for the Mahatma,* 1955; *The Financial Expert,* 1956; *The Guide,* 1958; *The Man-eater of Malgudi,* 1959 (all novels); *Astrologer's Day and Other Stories (short stories),* 1947; etc.

Narvane, V.S.

Essayist, Assistant Professor of Philosophy, Allahabad University; Publications; *Rabindranath Tagore : A Philosophical Study;* etc.

Panigrahi, Kalindicharan

Oriya novelist, playwright and poet; Member, Executive. Board of Sahitya Akademi; Publications; *Matira Mansha; Luhar Manisha,* (both novels); etc.

Panjwani, Ram

Sindhi poet, novelist and folklorist; Professor of Sandhi, Jai Hind College. Bandra, Bombay, 1948; Publications; *Qalidi,* 1943; *Chandi Jo Chamko,* 1947; *Zindagi Ya Maut,* 1952; Ahe-Na-Ahe, 1956 (all novels); *Sindhi Kalam, Sind Ji Sookhri* (anthologies). 1948-1952; etc.

Panikkar, K.M.

Author and historian in Malayalam and English; was

India's Ambassador to China, Egypt and France; Member of Parliament (1959-61); Vice-chancellor, Jammu & Kashmir University; Publications; *Asia and Western Dominance; A Survey of Indian History;* and several volumes of verse and drama in Malayalam.

Parekh, Nagindas

Gujarati Biographer and translator; was Professor in Gujarat Vidyapeeth of Mahatma Gandhi; has edited several journal and translated many works to Tagore in Gujarati.

Pillai, Thakazhi Sivasankara

Malayalam novelist and short-story writer; Winner of Akademi Award; Publications; *Thottiude Makan,* 1948; Rantitangazhi, 1949; *Chemmen,* 1956 (all novels); etc.

Pritam, Amrita (Smt.)

Punjabi poetess and novelist; winner of the Akademi Award; Publications; *Lamia Vatan, poetry, 1948; Pinjar,* novel, 1950; *Sunehure,* poetry, 1955; etc.

Pushp, P.N.

Kashmiri essayist and orientalist. Research Officer, Publications Divisions, Srinagar; Publications; *Kashmiri Sahitya;* An Anthology of *Kashmiri Verse.*

Puttappa, K.V.

Kannada poet, dramatist and essayist; Padmabhushana; Winner of Akademi Award; was Vice-Chancelor of Mysore University; Publications; 50 books in Kannada, notably biographies of Ramakrishna and Vivekananda and *Shri Ramayana Darshanam* (epic).

Rahi Rahman

Kashmiri poet and essayist; Edited *Kwang Pash,* the

first literary magazine in Kashmiri for 3 years. Secretary, Kashmir Cultural Congress; Publications : Sanawani Saz *Subhuk Sada, Nawraz Saba* (poems).

Raut Roy, Sachhidanand

Oriya poet. novelist and short-story writer; Participated in International Seminar of Arts and Sciences in Harvard University, 1955; Publicatons : *Chitrangada* (novel, 1937); *Baji Raut,* 1941; *Pandulipi,* 1946 (poems), *Masanir Phul* (short stories), 1946; *The Bootman Boy and Forty Poems,* 1954.

Reddi, B. Gopala

Telugu poet and critic : Minister, Union Government; President. Andhra Sahitya Akademi; has published several translations of Tagore's plays and poems : *Visarjana,* 1943; *Chitrangada,* 1945; *Malini,* 1954; *Urvasi,* 1953; *Kalidasa,* 1954; etc.

Sen, Sukumar

Bengali linguist and historian of literature : Khaira Professor of India Linguistics and Phonetics and Head of the Department of Comparative Philology, Calcutta University; Fellow of the Asiatic Society (1951); Member, Executive Board. Sahitya Akademi; Publications; *A History of Brajabuli Literature,* 1935; *Comparative Grammar of Middle Indo-Aryan,* 1951; *History and Pre-History of Sanskrit,* 1957; *History of Bengali Literature* (in Bengali, 4 volumes, 1940-1958; in English, 1960); etc.

Shastri, Gaurinath

Sanskrit scholar and specialist on Navya-Nyaya, Principal Sanskrit College, Calcutta.

Somasundaram, MI, PA.

Tamil poet and novelist; was editor of *kalki;* at present literary Producer, A.I.R., Madras; President. Tamil Writers' Association, 1959; Publications; *Ravi Chandrika* (novel), *Aindorir* (Fine Arts of South India); etc.

Subbarao Rayaprolu

Telugu poet and essayist; was Professor of Telugu in Osmania and Tirupati Universities, President of Navya Sahitya Parishad. 1924-40; Publictions; *Trin Kankanamu,* 1913; *Ramyalokamu,* 1937 (poems) : *City of Orungal,* 1943; *Vemana,* 1957. etc.

Suroor, Ale Ahmad

Urdu poet and critic; Head of the Department of Urdu, Aligarh University; Member Executive Board of Sahitya Akademi; Publications: *Safsabil: Zauke Junoon* (poems); *Abad Aur Nazariya* (criticism); etc.

Warerkar. B.V. (Mama)

Marathi dramatist and novelist; Padmabhushana; Member of Parliament; Member, Executive Board of Sahitya Akademi; has published over forty plays and several volumes of novels and short stories; has translated many works of Bankim Chandra and Tagore in Marathi.

To conclude, the Akademi had to take a hasty decision regarding this special Tagore Centenary Award. Infact the decision to institute the Award was taken in August 1961, recommendations received and the Award declared and presented in November 1961. Neveretheless, the Akademi not only did justice to these Tagore scholars, but was also in keeping with its object to encourage "Men of promise in letters" by giving away such prizes or other distinctions to writers of merit.

4
BIRTH ANNIVERSARY OF TAGORE

Every year the Birth Anniversary of Rabindranath Tagore that falls on 7th May is celebrated with great enthusiasm by the Sahitya Akademi in collaboration with Lalit Kala Akademi, Sangeet Natak Akademi and the Bengal Association at Rabindra Bhavan, New Delhi. Some common features of this celebration are the presentation of songs of Tagore by the exponents of Rabindra Sangeet and the display of Tagore paintings at the Exhibition Hall. In one of the preceding chapters, the Birth Centenary of Rabindranath has been discussed at length. Here we document only few memorable events. To mark the 105th Birth Anniversary of Gurudev, the three Akademies of Sahitya, Sangeet Natak and Lalit Kala jointly organised a brief but well attended function in which the gift of a portrait of the poet was formally received. It was held at Rabindra Bhavan, New Delhi on 7th May 1966 that began with the recital of a traditional Tagore birthday song (written by the poet on 23 Vaishakh 1348 (1940) and sung by Smt. Rita Chatterjee entitled 'He Nutan'

"He nutan
dekha dīk ār-bār janmer pratham śubhakśaṇ
tomar prakaś hok kuhelika kari udghātan
suryer matan/
riktatār bakśa bhedi āpanāre karo unmochan
byakta hok jībaner jay

byakta hok tomāmājhe asīmer chirabismay
udaydigante śaṅkha bāje, mor chittamajhe
chiranutanere dito dāk
pamchīśe baiśākh//"

"May the first auspicious moment of birth
Appear again, O Forever New.
May your spirit rise through the mists
of twilight like the sun.
Unfold yourself piercing the bosom of utter perdition.
May the glory of life incarnate
May the eternal wonder of the limitless configure in you.
When the conch shell rings from the horizon of sunrise.
It sends through my heart a call
To the forever new the 25th of baisakh

After this, Savitri Chatterjee sung three more songs of Rabindranath.

A portrait of Tagore done by an eminent Iranian artist Mr.. Akbar Tajvidi was presented on behalf of the Iranian Embassy in India by its Cultural Counsellor Mr. Mahmoud Tafazzoli and was received by Sri. S.N. Mozumdar, Vice-Chairman, Sangeet Natak Akademi on behalf of the three Akademies. The portrait was based on a photograph taken during the poet's sojourn to Iran. An excellent specimen of the classical Iranian design and handiwork, the portrait is done on artistically cut ivory and framed with Iranian style illumination in an inlaid frame of 53cm x 43 cm.

Mr. Tafazzoli in his speech spoke about the growing

interest of the Iranian people in Indian art and culture. He said that when at the age of 71 Rabindranath accepted an invitation of the late Shah of Iran to visit that country in 1932, he became the first ambassador of the new India to Iran.

A novel feature of this celebration was the presentation of Persian version of 'Gitanjali' one of the many published in Iran and two copies of a special number of the Review of the Arts Faculty. Tahran University, which was published on the occasion of the Tagore Centenary in 1961. One may recall that Mr. Mahmoud Tafazzoli himself was an astute translator who rendered Jawahar Lal Nehru's works into Persian.

While thanking Mr. Tafazzoli and the Government of Iran for the portrait and the other gifts, Sri S.N. Mozumdar referred to the close bonds of cultural and linguistic alliance which had existed from time immemorial between Iran and India.

Rabindranath Tagore, Sri Mozumdar said, was once hailed by an Iranian poet thus :

The caravans of India always carry sugar.
But this time it has the perfume of the muse.
Oh caravan! please stop your march,
Because burning hearts are following thee
Like the butterflies which burn
Around the flame of candles

Again on 9th May the three National Akademies organised a special function at Rabindra Bhavan, under the chairmanship of Dr. B. Gopala Reddi.

Dr. R.K. Dasgupta of the Delhi University spoke about Tagore's image in India. The major attractions of the evening were the rendering of Rabindra Sangeet by the renowned singer Hemanta Mukhopadhyay and flute recitical by Sri Devendra Murdeshwar.

On May 15, at a special ceremony, held at Rabindra Bhavan, New Delhi, The Sangeet Natak Akademi again paid homage to the memory of Rabindranath, when a few tape recorded songs of Tagore were played.

They were sung by Srimati Sahana Devi, one of the greatest exponents of Tagore music.

On the occasion of 120th Birth Anniversary of Rabindranath Tagore, the Regional office at Madras arranged a programme on 5 May 1980 under the Chairmanship of Sri. P. Padmaraju. Dr. B. Gopala Reddi spoke on the many sided personality of Tagore.

To celebrate the 125th Birth Anniversary of Tagore, various programmes were planned by the Akademi. On 9 May 1986 the Prime Minister, Sri Rajiv Gandhi inaugurated a three-day celebration, organised by the Ministry of Human Resource Development at Tin Murti House, New Delhi. The President of the Sahitya Akademi, Prof. V.K. Gokak, presented the key-note address on *"A new world perspective for reading of Tagore's poetry."* On the occasion, a book on Rabindranath Tagore written by Prof. Sisir Kumar Ghose and published by the Sahitya Akademi was also released.

It was followed by recitation of Tagore's poems by veteran Bengali stage personality Sri Shombhu Mitra.

On the following two evenings three plays of Tagore were staged.

Durasha and *Rakta Karabi* directed by Smt. Tripti Mitra of Arabddha Natya Vidyalay, Calcutta was staged on 10th May 1986 at Sri Ram Centre Auditorium, College Road (now Safdar Hashmi Marg), Mandi House, New Delhi. The narrative structure of Tagore's short story, "Durasha"

(Impossible Hope) is that of a woman telling her life story to a Bengali writer. The writer meets the woman in Darjeeling on a cold and foggy day in 1896. She is the daughter of Gulam Qader Khan, the Nawab of Budraun. She now describes herself as Musalmani-Brahmani (i.e. a Muslim-Brahmin). It is this transition that the story seeks to explore. The cast comprised of

Narrator	:	Alo Gupta
Writer	:	Sudip Kar
Sanyasini	:	Tripti Mitra
Light	:	Tapas Sen
Set	:	Khaled Chowdhury
Music	:	Tarit Bhattacharya
Direction	:	Tripti Mitra

The next production was Tagore's *Rakta Karabi* (Red Oleanders). Tripi Mitra, the Director of 'Arabddhya Natya Vidyalay' stated : After Bohurupee stopped producing Rakta Karabi people seemed to have forgotten the play. It is a great pity because I do think that it needed being staged before the public. Its relevance has, if anything, increased in today's confused and frightening world. The poet had foreseen the evil forces which have come to the fore. As he himself wrote in Red Oleanders : (Author's Interpretation)

"I feet that this message needs to be spread to the present generation, for which task who could be better suited than representatives of this generation, new and young actors and actresses" The young cast comprised of

Nandini	:	Angana Basu
Digger Boy (Kishore)	:	Pradip Chakraborty
Professor (Adhyapak)	:	Susanta Das
Gokul	:	Sudip Kar

King (Raja)	:	Satinath Mukhopadhyay
Chandra	:	Rwita Chakraborty
Phagulal	:	Alo Gupta
Bishu	:	Soumyadeb Basu
Governor (Sardar)	:	Sudrshan Chakraborty
Preacher (Gosain)	:	Tapas Manna
Head man (Modal)	:	Kallol Chakraborty
Assistant Governor (Chhoto Sardar)	:	Banikantha Bagain
Antiquarian (Puran Bagis)	:	Gokul Mitra
Gajju (Wrestler)	:	Kallol Chakraborty
Doctor	:	Gokul Mitra
Head Man No. 321	:	Sanat Kumar Dawn
Deputy Governor (Mejo Sardar)	:	Arun Dutta
Gokul's Party	:	Kallol Chakraborty Tapas Manna Arup Manna
The Bearers	:	Gokul Mitra, Debashis Chatterjee, Pradip Chakraborty, Banikantha Bagani, Sanat Kumar Dawn.
Off Stage	:	Mukti Chakraborty, Rupa Kar, Lily Chakraborty, Merina Bibi, Biswajit Prasad, Dulal Sinha, Joy Sen, Uday De, Durga Prasad Rao, Biswanath Mondal.

Lights	:	Tapas Sen
Background Music	:	Tarit Bhattacharya
Set	:	Khaled Chowdhury
Direction	:	Tripti Mitra

'Chitrangada' was presented by Visva-Bharati, Shantiniketan on 11 May 1986, at Kamani Auditorium, Copernicus Marg, New Delhi. 'Chitrangada' the original drama in verse, was composed in 1892. It was rendered into English by the Poet himself in 1913 under the title 'Chitra' The original drama in verse was recast in its present form in 1936 by the Author. The version described by him was *Nritya-Natya Chitrangada.* (Dance-drama Chitrangada). This dance-drama was presented for the first time on board the New Empire Theatre, Calcutta in March 1936, the poet being present on the stage. The story of Chitrangada arises out of a legend in the Mahabharata; telling how Arjuna, wandering in fulfilment of a vow of penance, came to Manipur, and fell in love with Chitrangada, only daughter of the King. She because her father had no male heir, had received a boy's education, and been treated in all ways as a son. Arjuna married her on the understanding that should they have a son, he should be regarded not as the descendant of his race, but as the propitiator of the royal line of Manipur. He lived with Chitrangada for three years : and when their child was born, he embraced her finally and setout again on his travels.

This rather dry tale has been used by the Poet in much the same way as Shakespeare used the older plays and stories upon which he founded his dramas; that is, as a point of departure rather than as a plot. Little of it survives in his poem beyond the names of the characters and the Amazonian character of Chitrangada herself.

In the present Visva-Bharati production, the Chorus

was led by great Rabindra Sangeet exponent Smt. Kanika Banerji.

All these plays received encomiums and appreciation from the theatre audience of Delhi.

A National Seminar on Tagore was also organised from 28th to 30th August 1986. It was inaugurated by Sri Thakazi Sivasankara Pillai at the Triveni Auditorium, New Delhi and presided over by Prof. V.K. Gokak. Sri Krishna Kripalani graced the occasion and gave a short lecture. 'Rabigeetika' presented a programme of songs and poems of Tagore.

A reprint of Sahitya Akademi's publication 'Rabindranath Tagore : a centenary volume, 1861-1961' was released on the occasion. The seminar continued on 20th and 30th August in four sessions. As said earlier besides an usual variety cultural programmes, the Nobel Laureate is remembered every year in an informal literary forum meeting of the writers, scholars and intellectuals, 'Rabindranath Tagore Remembered', is a programme that was held at New Delhi on 8 May 1994, on 7 May 1995 and also on 5 May 1996 to celebrate 136th Birth Anniversary.

5
TAGORE SEMINARS, WORKSHOPS & LITERARY FORUMS

It was envisaged in 1955 to have a seminar on Rabindranath Tagore, a natural choice owing to the 100th anniversary of the birth of Rabindranath Tagore which was to fall in 1961. From the very beginning, the Sahitya Aacdemy has organised many Seminars at International, National, Regional and local level on a variety of subjects of literary interests and also on select literary luminaries. This is one of the main activities of the Akademi to provide a common forum for writers and scholars. Some of these Seminars were organised in association with important institutions and organisations in India and abroad. Sahitya Akademi has organised four significant Tagore Seminars at different levels. The very first one was an International Seminar to mark the Birth Centenary of Rabindranath in 1961. Again on the occasion of his 125th Birth Anniversary, at National level a Seminar was held from 7th to 9th August 1991, a three days long Seminar entitled *"Tagore's Vision of India : Its Relevance Today"* was organised Presently Sahitya Akademi is also having a series of discussions on select Indian Classics. The series of discussions on select Indian Classics. The first classic taken up was Rabindranath Tagore's *Gora*. The first Seminar in the series was held on 21 April 1933 in Bombay, followed by Literary Forum Seminar on *Gora* again on 30 April at New Delhi and on 19 June at Hampi.

(I) International Literary Seminar to Mark the Birth Centenary of Rabindranath Tagore (12th-14th November 1961)

As part of the Tagore Centenary Celebrations in India, the Shitya Akademi in collaboration with the Indian Council for Cultural Relations and with the assistance of UNESCO, organised a three days International Literary Seminar from 12th to 14th November 1961 at New Delhi.

Its inauguration by Dr. S. Radhakrishnan, Vice-President of India, on November 11, 1961, marked the first major event of the Tagore Week in Delhi which was inaugurated at the same time. The Seminar was attended by several scholars, intellectuals, writers and academies. In all, 39 Indian delegates representing 16 languages of India and 25 distinguished writers from 16 foreign countries participated in this Seminar, held at Vigyan Bhavan, New Delhi.

Given below the list of Indian delegates in the alphabetical order of the languages represented :–

Assamese	:	Dr. Birinchi Kumar Barua
		Sri Hem Barua
		Sri Nabakanta Barua
Bengali	:	Sri Prabhat Kumar Mukherji
		Sri Premendra Mitra
		Dr. Sukumar Sen
English	:	Dr. Bhabani Bhattaharya
		Dr. Mulk Raj Anand
		Sri R.K. Narayan
Gujarati	:	Sri Kakasaheb Kalelkar
		Sri Nagindas Parekh

		Sri Umashankar Joshi
Hindi	:	Dr. Hazari Prasad Dwivedi
		Sri Jainendra Kumar
		Sri Ramdhari Sinha 'Dinkar'
Kannada	:	Sri Adhya Rangacharya
Kashmiri	:	Prof. J.L. Kaul
		Prof. P.N. Pushp
Malayalam	:	Sri Thakazhi Sivasankara Pillai
Marathi	:	Sri B.V. Warerkar (Mama Warerkar)
		Smt. Kusumavati Deshpande
		Dr. V.S. Naravane
Oriya	:	Sri Kalindicharan Panigrahi
		Dr. Mayadhar Mansimha
		Sri Sochi Rautray
Punjabi	:	Smt. Amrita Pritam
		Sri Balwant Gargi
		Prof. Mohan Singh
Sanskrit	:	Dr. Suniti Kumar Chatterji
Sindhi	:	Sri Jairamdas Doulatram
		Prof. L.H. Ajwani
		Prof. Ram Panjwani
Tamil	:	Dr. A.C. Chettiar
		Prof. K. Chandra Sekharan
Telugu	:	Sri B. Gopala Reddi
		Sri Rayaprolu Subbarao
Urdu	:	Prof. A.A. Suroor

Prof. Ehtesham Husain

Dr. Masud Husain Khan

Name of the foreign delegates are presented here in the alphabetical order of their countries :

Ceylon	:	Mr. Martin Wickremesinghe
Czechoslovakia	:	Dr. Dusan Zbavitel
France	:	Mr. Jean Cuehenno
Germany (East)	:	Mr. H. Krueger
		Mr. Walter Ruben
Germany (West)	:	Mr. Hans Erich Nossack
		Dr. Rudolf Hagelstange
Iran	:	Dr. Lutfali Suratgar
Japan	:	Madame Tomiko Kora
		Madame Yoko Matsuo-Ka
League of Arab States	:	Mr. Clovis Maksoud
		Madame Khashab
		Dr. Yehya al Khashab
Sweden	:	Prof. H.S. Nyberg
Thailand	:	H.H. Prince Prem Purachatra
U.A.R.	:	Dr. Zaki Naguib Mahmoud
U.K.	:	Mr. Aldous Muxley
		Sri Isaiah Berlin
U.S.A.	:	Mr. Louis Untermeyer
U.S.S.R.	:	Mr. E.P. Chelyshev
		Madame Nobikova
		Mr. Vsevolod Ivonov
Yogoslavia	:	Mr. Josep Vidmar
		Mr. Joze Javozseka Brejc

From Unesco, Mr. Djoehana had graced this great literary even Seven renowned delegates from abroad had to cancel their visit to the Seminar for reasons of health. They were Madame Victoria Ocampo from Argentina, H.E.M. Andre Malraux and M. Andre Maurois of France, Mr. Archibald Macleish of the United States, Mr. Leonid Sobolev of U.S.S.R. Dr. Carl Zuckmayer of West-Germany and Mr. Ivo Andric of Yugoslavia.

The Seminar was inaugurated by Dr. S. Radhakrishnan. Vice-President of Indian on 11 November 1961 and continued till 14 November 1961. It may be added here that on the occasion of the inauguration of the International Literary Seminar, a comprehensive Tagore Centenary Volume in English was formally released by him. Dr. Radhakrishnan, in his address, recalled Hegel's remarks that "Persia is the land of light, Greece of grace. Rome of empire and India of dream." "The greatest gift of life is the dream of a higher, a better, a nobler life...(Tagore's) aspiration held a better life to overcome the conflict which is in ourselves. The duality, there is so much also which deserves horror and contempt, to integrate human nature to find out how what the theologians call the home duplex can be made into single mindedness that is the problem by which we are faced and Tagore tells us—*Obstinate are the trammels but my heart aches when I try to break them. The shroud that covers me is a shroud of dust and death; I hate it yet I hug it in love.'... If the human individual is able to liberate himself from the compulsions of nature from the strains of history, he can displace within his own self and feel that he can supersede nature, manipulate nature, transform it, then he becomes a real creator. As a poet, Tagore felt that his purpose was to tell human beings that they have in them the power... to transform nature itself and transform history... Rabindranath's life and work bear witness to the ultimate hope that despite vast errors man kind has its justification."*

After the inaugural address, foreign delegates delivered their speeches and messages. Themes chosen for the discussions were :–

1. *Rabindranath Tagore and Modern Indian Literature*
2. *Rabindranath Tagore and the World*
3. *Literature and Modern Life*

The first theme dealt chiefly with Tagore's influence on the formative period in the various literatures of contemporary India. The Second discussed the impact of his personality and writings outside India and his contribution to the building of a better understanding between the different countries and cultures of the world. The third subject was of a general natural and discussed the relation between life and literature, and in particular the impact of modern knowledge and technological development on contemporary letters.

Several papers were read which were followed by discussion under the Chairmanship of Sri Humayun Kabir, Minister for Scientific Research and Cultural Affairs Enlisted below is the papers presented by the distinguished scholars :–

1. Calamawi, Sahair El. Facing problems in education with the poet Tagore
2. Chelyshew, E. Rabindranath Tagore in the Soviet Union.
3. Kora, Tomiko. Tagore and Japan
4. Matsuoka, Yoko. Tagore and Japan
5. Nyberg, H.S. Tagore and the world : significance of the work of Rabindranath.
6. Purachatra, Prem. Tagore and the world.

7. Tucci, Giuseppe. Tagore and the world : 'Tagore and the impact of modern life on contemporary writing.
8. Widmar, Josip, Rabindranath Tagore in Yogoslavia
9. Wickremesinghe, Martin. Tagore and Ceylon
10. Zbavitel, Dusan Rabindrantha Tagore and Czechoslovakia.
11. Zuchmayer, Carl. Rabindranath Tagore and Germany

Let's summarize the deliberations of the Seminar with special emphasis on the contributions made by the paper readers.

Sahair El Calamawi spoke on Tagore's essays directly bearing an educational problems. He makes a short survey to mention several problems in education in India and in his homeland, and see them with the poet's eye. He started with the first and foremost problem of Professors, as Tagore rightly observes that the relation of Professors to students is a main factor in education. The cult of the "gurus in India is quite similar to the cult of "Sheikhs" in Arab civilization. Up till the middle of the last century direct contact with the teacher was the only form of education known to us. Calamawi also dealt with shortage of teachers, material means and appropriate atmosphere for learning. Tagore's main purpose in forming the "Shantiniketan" was creating an atmoshpere which he described in saying *"I tried to create an atmosphere in my shcool—this was the main task. In educational institutions our faculties have to be nourished in order to give our mind its freedom, to make our imagination fit for the world which belongs to art, and to stir our sympathy for human relationships. This last is even more important from learning the geography of foreign lands."*

The scholar opines that had Tagore not been a true poet, his educational ideas may have been neglected.

E. Chelyshev stated that Tagore effected a real revolution in the literature and art of his people, made a tremendous, invaluable contribution to the development of world civilization, and laid a firm foundation for the friendship and mutual understanding of the peoples of the Soviet Union and India, Chalyshev recalls Tagore's "Letter about Russia" which played a tremendous role in strengthening friendship and mutual understanding between the peoples of India and the U.S.S.R. He adds we also deeply value Tagore for the sympathy which, when dying and featured to his bed, he showed for the great liberating war of the Soviet people against the fascist aggressors."

Tomiko Kora in the paper 'Tagore and Japan' says "Rabindranath Tagore's most unforgettable influence on the Japanese thought-life was his well-thought-out criticism on Japanese militaristic inclinations towards her Asain brothers, and her two hasty industrialisation based upon narrow nationalism of the time. His words were really prophetic to the fate of Japan. His warnings proved true in the following 30 years of Asian History. His second and third visit to Japan proved his deep love for our people and long standing culture and art. However, to our grave sorrow, his expectation on Japan was betrayed on the occasion of Japan's waging war over China, down to the South Asian countries, even to Indian Assam, under the name of liberation Asia; thus causing war against the U.S.A. and the world powers in the world war II. The notorious Atom-Bombing on Hiroshima and Nagasaki took place after the death of Rabindranath Tagore who had left "crisis of civilisation" on his disheartened bed and gone!! Yoko Matsuoka while speaking on Tagore and Japan informs "It was only after we experienced the war and the defeat that

Tagore's thoughts have come to be really understood. Now we can look back to the famous Tagore—Naguchi bout with perspective and appreciation. His Nationalism is now read with a different frame of mind. A new wave in the introduction of Tagore's works since 1958 indicates a kind of interests and appreciation heretofore not existed. The recent translation of Romain Rolland's Indian Diary also helped to arouse interests among a much wider circle of people than previously possible. Many of us are now able to share the feeling so eloquently expressed by Tagore during his visit to China : '*Let all human races keep their personalities and yet come together, not in a uniformity that is dead, but in a unity that is living ;*" H.S. Nyberg in his paper 'Tagore and the world : significance of the work of Rabindranath Tagore' states "very little was known of the poetry of Rabindranath Tagore in 1913 when the attention of the Swedish Akademi, searching for a candidate of the Nobel Prize, was drawn by English admirers to the poet from far India then only represented by some of the earliest English translations. They worked as a revelation. One of the members of the Akademi, Verner von Heidenstam, one of our most famous poets and himself later a Nobel Prize winner, felt at once the strong lyrical inspiration, the beauty and the profound and generous humanity of this poetry which betrayed a truly great poet. He told the Akademi : 'Quite as a mere selection of Goethe's poems would suffice to convince us of Goethe's grandeur, even if the rest of his work were not familiar to us, in the same way we can say that the poetry of Tagore which we have seen this summer (1913) has revealed to us one of the greatest poets of our time. I have read it with emotion, and I can not remember having met, since decades of years, anything in lyric literature that might be measured with this festivals of the spirit which only might be compared with drinking fresh and limpid water of a spring. The ardent and tender religious sentiment by which his thoughts and feelings are permeated, the purity of his heart and the sublimity of his style, noble and natural at the same time, are fused into a unity of a rare and profound beauty. There is in it nothing debatable, nothing contused, nothing related to the vanities of this world, no narrowness of mind; and if ever there has been a poet of whom it could really be said that he possesses the qualities which justify a Nobel Prize, it is certainly Rabindranath Tagore." Scholar Prem Purachatra in his paper entitled *"Tagore and the world"* states "No Indian writer of modern times is so well known to us as Rabindranath Tagore. His works have been translated into Thai and are therefore known beyond the group of educated persons who are well versed in English. Songs from *Gitanjali* are to be found in the Thai version. Of his plays. *Chitra* is perhaps the most widely familiar, although *The Post Office* and *The King of the Dark Chamber* are also appreciated... The works of Rabindranath Tagore are recognised by the Thai people as having a universal appeal. His philosophic wisdom and humanitarian ideals are held in high regard. His concept of the brotherhood of man is well appreciated. The spiritual undertone of his creative genius is shared by our people, who regards him as a symbol of renascent Asia backed by centuries of culture."

Josip Vidmar in "*Rabindranath Tagore in Yogoslavia*" opines : There is only one poet in European literature comparable to Tagore with regard to understanding of nature. It is the great pantheist Goethe. And yet, what a difference! In Goethe nearly every deep contact with nature is permeated by his will, by mental striving after understanding and knowledge. Goethe penetrates into nature, Tagore's heart opens to it and he sees "the world immersed into wonderful brightness, washed from all sides of waves of beauty and joy", as he himself describes his first experience of this kind in his memoirs. And if Goethe in his attitude towards nature represents Europe—which he indubitably does–then Tagore is something different. Perhaps it is a daring thought, yet let us express it–Tagore is Asia or India, and also, if you wish, the female principle of spirituality compared to the male of Goethe. He is tender and yet powerful and charming as Goethe is powerful and mighty in his manifestations. Two worlds, complementing each other."

Was Tagore a mystic? Giuseppe Tucci in his paper *'Tagore and the universal man'* answers "He was, and he was not. He was a mystic in the sense that he perceived and endeavoured to realize within himself a presence which is beyond the common experience, but at the sometime he was concerned with the same everyday problems with which common men are concerned. He was an educationist, according to the more modern lines, he had his clear ideas about the organisation of village life, he anticipated the role which Indian was to play in the international balance, he insisted on that universal co-operation, failing which mankind is likely to revert to a state of barbarism but his readiness to appraise the new situation, his attempts to find out new direction in social life, all this was not based on merely theoretically economical, or political urges. Life is here, a divine boon, and we must make the best of it, for ourselves and for our fellowmen, but social life too not a tree without a root. The root is that which imparts life and energy to the whole tree. The visible has a foundation in the invisible... beyond everyday life, beyond the clarity of science which kills every sparkle of the divine in us, beyond life and death, there lies something which we do not know, which we shall never know, but we feel as the eternal immutable sources of whatever flows in time. There lies the origin of our being, the reason of the equality of our nature, the sameness in destiny, the only unknown thing, the contemplation of whose mystery can given some sense to the brief transit from birth to death, which we call life.

This is the menage that Tagore has left us, and in which we can still find an inspiration, and the urge to restore that balance between mind and spirit which threatens to collapse."

Louis Untermeyer in the short essay *'Tagore and the impact of modern life on contemporary writing"* recalls that Tagore foretold the effect of a power—drien, power-mad civilization. He even envisioned the spectre of the atom bomb. "In this whole universe," write Tagore :

The giant wheel of pain revolves
Stars and planets split up;
Sparks of fiery dust speed and intensify
The anguish of existence.

Untermeyer added that if contemporary writing has been adversely affected by present daily technology with its power to disturb and destroy, it has also benefitted from that destructiveness.

The impact of modern life has, to a considerable extent, destroyed what is false infact and spurious in fiction; it has made us turn away from a specious romanticism to take a hard look at reality."

Martin Wickremesinghe in *'Tagorea and Ceylon'* points out that inspired by Tagore's *Sapa Mochana* they have independently developed their own mudranataka or dance drama. The recent development of Buddhist folk drama is not due to the direct influence of Tagore's *Sapa Mochana'*. In 1934 Rabindranath visited Ceylon and his dance-drama made a deep impression on the intelligentsia.

Dusan Zbavitel in the paper *'Rabindranath Tagore and Czechoslovakia'* spoke on the influence of Rabindranath

Tagore on the increase of interest in India, generally, and on the development of indological studies abroad. From this point of view, Rabindranath's personality, poetry and activities are of such a significance that he can hardly be compared with any of his contemporaries in India. Czechoslovakia is a good example of how the horizon of indology was widened after Rabindranath Tagore had given the impulse and raised a new interest in modern Indian Culture among Czech public. In Dusan Zbavitel's works "It was Rabindranath's well-known ideas about the receiving of establishment of peace in the world which appeal to our very hearts nowadays as strongly as they did in those times when they were proclaimed by the Poet... he stood against fascism wherever it had seized power, in Spain as well as in Italy, in Japan as well as in Germany; "This devastating tide of international fascism must be checked"; he proclaimed on the 2nd March, 1937 in his statement on the situation in Spain... Czechoslovakia was one of those countries which fell victim to the fascism and had to suffer under the Nazi oppression for long six years. No wonder, then, that we are not willing to forget that terrible experience. Neither shall we forget however, those who proved to be true friends of our country in that critical time and who boldly condemned the treachery of Munich perpetrated by the Western Powers which put Czechoslovakia at the mercy of Hitler. In this sense, Rabindranath's open letter to Prof. Lesny published on the 10th November, 1938, will always remain in our memories as an unforgettable document of his true friendship as well as of his noble humanism" Carl Zuchmayer in his paper titled *"Rabindranath Tagore and Germany"* putforth a fascinating true story from the first world was in which he himself took part as a young German soldier. A friend of his who was a sergeant in the medical corps told it to him. Zuchmayer narrates :

"...To the Front hospital in which he worked as an assistant surgeon they brought one day an Indian soldier who has been taken prisoner after he was badly wounded in both legs. There was no other chance to save his life than an immediate amputation of one of his legs. But for this purpose the chief surgeon wanted the consent or at least the confidence of the wounded man. The Indian soldier who served with a 'Gurkha-Regiment' in the British army spoke no German, of course, and his English was rather unintelligible; moreover, the German medical officers knew little English. So there was almost no chance for a mutual understanding, and the more they tried, the more our poor Indian soldier grew fearful and anxious (God knows what he had been told before about the cruelty of the enemies, for he believed that they were going to kill him or to do him some other serious harm). It was then that my friend who was a student of medicine and one of those Germans who are more 'learned' than 'belligerent' thought of the only Indian word, or name, he knew-it was the name of the Indian poet who had won the Nobel Prize in 1913 : Rabindranath Tagore. So he bent down his head to the Indian who lay in the cold sweat of fear and whispered in his ear this name : Rabindranath Tagore; Rabindranath Tagore! Rabindrana Tagore! After he had said it three times the Indian seemed to understand. His face relaxed, a shy little smile came into his eyes, then he closed them, his fear was gone, and he nodded weakly his consent and confidence to the enemy doctors.

I felt touched by this unpretentious little story for it seemed to me to hold a peculiar significance : what a name, a single name, can mean as a bridge of understanding and faith between man."

Above were the extractors from various papers

contributed by distinguished writers and scholars on the occasion. The concluding session of the Seminar was open to public and was addressed by Mr. Aldous Huxley, Sir Isaiah Berlin (from the U.K.), Madam Yoko Matsuoka (from Japan), M. Jean Guehenno (from France), Prince Prem Purachatra (from Thailand), Mr. Vsevolod Ivonov (from U.S.S.R.), Mr. Hans Erich Nossack (from Germany) and Mr. Josep Vidmar from Yugoslavia.

Aldous Huxley spoke on Tagore's ideas on education which were essentially humanistic. In his words 'Tagore was attempting to realise human potentialities in their fullness. He realised very clearly and we can see this in his various educational essays that education at it stands at present suffers from a grave defect, that it is primarily an education in terms of words and concepts. He saw that children were being trained in the use of words and that the whole conceptional side of their mind was being educated but the non-verbal side of the human being was being neglected.

He saw that it was necessary to train not only the word using, the concept–using part of the mind but also to train the perception, the imagination and the body in general, the whole muscular apparatus. Without this kind of universal training the child would grow up into a lopsided individual. And he summed up these ideas in a phrase which I quoted during the Seminar and which I wish to quote here again. He said :

Man for his perfection must be vitally savage, mentally civilised and he added :

The proportion the savage to the civilised should be roughly what the proportion of sea to earth is on our planet.

And he perceived that the man has in his totality a greater extent, a greater volume of savage, irrational,* nonlogical elements that he has conceptualised logical elements and that if we want to produce integrated human beings, we must accept this fact and train the human being on the non-verbal irrational level to exactly the same extent that we train him on the conceptual and verbal level."

**(Irrational may be interpreted to mean non-rational which includes both the irrational and the suprarational)*

The concluding session was presided over by Dr. S. Radhakrishnan who in his concluding address stressed upon the civilising nature of education. He said vital dynamism, intellectual efficiency and spiritual development constituted the proper aim of education. The civilisation of the future would embrace all the values of the civilisations that had come together. Tagore pleaded for this light of humanity, and he was convinced, being an optimist, that this light of humanity would dispense the dark and menacing clouds.

A select references to newspaper reviews presented here would speak for itself the media's exuberance and enthusiasm with Tagore Seminar.

"Impact of Tagore on modern literature" *Indian Express* (New Delhi); 13 Nov. 1961.

Make world happy home for humanity : call to writers at Tagore Centenary Literary Seminar". *Amrita Bazar Patrika* (Calcutta); 15 Nov. 1961.

"Respond to changes of time : Dr. Radhakrishnan's call to writers. "*The Mail* (Madras); 15 Nov. 1961.

"Tagore : a great internationalist" *Deccan Herald* (Bangalore); 12 Nov. 1961.

"Tagore gave life to east-west theory : International Seminar Studies poet's role". *Indian Express* (New Delhi); 14 Nov. 1961.

"Tagore's impact on Indian literature : experiments in education interest Huxley". *The Hindustan Stadard* (Calcutta); 13 Nov. 1961.

"Tagore's love of humanity praised : Radhakrishnan inaugurates literary conference." *The Mail* (Madras); 12 Nov. 1961.

"Tagore's work at Shantiniketan : Aldous Huxley points out a lession in education". *The Satesman.* (New Delhi); 14 Nov. 1961.

"World delegates pay homage to Tagore". *Time of India* (New Delhi); 13 Nov. 1961.

The nation wide celebrations of Tagore Birth Centenary concluded with this International Seminar organised by Sahitya Akademi, New Delhi.

(II) National Seminar on Rabindranath Tagore on the occasion of his 125th Birth Anniversary.

Twenty five years later the Sahitya Akademi organised the second Tagore Seminar, but this time at National level to mark the 125th Birth Anniversary of the poet. This as held at the Triveni Auditorium, New Delhi from 26 to 30 August 1986. The seminar was in augurated by veteran Malayam writer Sri. Thakazi Sivasankara. Pillai and presided over by Prof. V.K. Gokak, the President of Sahitya Akademi Sri Krishna Kripalani who was present on the occasion made a brief speech on the inaugural day, a reprint of Sahitya Academie's publication 'Rabindranath Tagore : a Centenary Volume (1861-1961) was released. Rabigeetikar presented a programme of songs and poem's of Tagore. On 26 August 1986 well known Hindi writer Amrit Rai delivered a lecture entitled '*Tagore : ever more relevant today*' in its Inaugural session. Amrit Rai in his long paper speaks of the dangerous game of nuclear one up manship that has brought the world to the present brink of total nuclear extinction. Nuclear destruction stares mankind in the face. It is indeed a very grim scenario as we meet here to celebrates the 125th Birth Anniversary of the poet" says Amrit Rai. He tells as a great humanity Tagore's paramount commitment is to life, to Man must and to Peace in the world. So we celebrate Rabindranath now because Rabindranath celebrates Life and the Joy of Life as probably no other poet does. That indeed is the essence of all his poetry.

The terms chosen for the seminar were :

1. *Rabindranath Tagore and Religion A Religion of Man;*
2. *Rabindranath Tagore and education : A Universal Concept;*
3. *Rabindranath Tagore and Literature, All Pervasive Excellence of Many Splendoured Genius*
4. *Rabindranath Tagore in Translation; Awaiting New Translators*

The First Session on 29 August 1986 was chaired by Prof. V.K. Gokak. Papers on the topic *'Rabindranath Tagore and Religion; A Religion of Man'* were presented by the following scholars :

Bandyopadhy, Asit. *A Religion of man.*

Barua, Nabakanta. *Tagore, religion of man : a poets faith.*

Bhattacharya, Debipada. *Rabindranath Tagore and religion : a religion of man.*

Das, Manoj *Tagore : the religion of man.*

Sri Bandyopadhyay in his paper *'A Religion of Man'* mentions : The Religion of Man is never a creedal religion, it is a Universal love, a path of eternal Bliss, the *'anada'* of the Upanishad... The whole world is born of bliss, the living creatures do live in bliss, and thence they retire to bliss. The religion of man is, therefore, the religion of Love which bring down the heaven to the earth and lifts the earth to the heaven. This is the main idea of religion of man presented by Tagore throughout his life, in his every form of artistic creations Nabakanta Barua States the Religion of Man, for Tagore is the world awareness of the self which is innate as well as achieved through conscious living which in turn is the ultimate human exemplar. Tagore achieved this totality in life and art. But he could not sit pretty with his achievement. Not Simply because he retrieved discarded flowers nor because he made discarded trends in the Indian reality the prime constituents of his faith, but because he maintained a constant confrontation with the self. He received jolts and had to undergo a nightmarish journey through doubt. But like the Hindu religion, his faith could absorb disparate elements of codes foreign to his make-up and yet remain his self... As the true poet, he does not have the prophetic tendency of falsifying experiences by adhering to certain tenets he had himself evolved, he is not to be trapped in his own web. His doubt is not what would perhaps lead to scientific discovery but is one that leads towards a more inclusive faith. In *'Rabindranath Tagore and religion : a religion of Man'* Sri Devipada Bhattacharya states that Bengal in the nineteenth century through western education was influenced by the writings of Bacon, Bentham, Thomas Paine, J.S. and Comte Darwin and Herbert Spencer also played a major role in shaping its young minds. The young Tagore was not unresponsive to those views. His intellectual faculty reached to those ideas. The three noble characters of his novels that he ever created, Jagamohan of 'Caturanga' (1915) Nikhilesh of "Ghare-Baire' (The home and the world) (1961) and Bipradas of 'Jogajog' (1929) are all nationalists and positivists. Rabindranath's ideal 'protagonists' are thus all humanists, free from practising any narrow sectarian religion Jagamohan, the noblest among the characters, is a God-denying 'atheist' who sacrifices his life while nursing the victims of a virulent epidemic in the slums for the downtrodden...

Tagore criticised strongly those religious customs, full of obscurantism obstructing the growth and fulfilment of human life. He visualised a world' *where the mind is without fear and the head is held high.* But in reality he saw un-reason, crude and repulsive elements over powering the true spirit of Religion..... in his poem, 'Bharat Tirtha' (1910) where the poet sends a clarion call to peoples of all races to unite irrespective of their religious faiths to merge into one Indian nation. This was his ideal of 'Universal Brotherhood of Man.' Manoj Das rightly regards Tagore as genius in creative literature. One who proves great in a certain sphere of inspired creativity, need not prove equally gifted in intellectual or philosophical exercises. But Tagore, apart from fitting into the Indian concept of the Kavi who is a seer too fell into the rare category of creative writers who were at the same time creative thinkers.

The second session was held on 29 August 1986 and was chaired by Prof. Nemai Sadhan Bose. The papers on the theme *'Rabindranath Tagore and Education : A Universal concept'* were presented by the following distinguished scholars.

Datta, Amlan Rabindranath Tagore's ideals of education.

Ghose, Sisir Kumar, Education in utopia.

Prema Nandakumar, Rabindranath Tagore and education.

Venugopal Rao, Pappu Rabindranath Tagore and education.

Sri Amlan Datta reconstructed his paper from a speech at the Special Assembly of the Dhaka Bengal Akademi on 24 May 1986. At the outset of his interesting paper, Sri Datta States' Man has drawn clear dividing lines between the useful and useless; the serious and non-serious, and although these lines are to be respected, the connections between the two must also be kept in mind. Nature is useful to us in many ways-giving us birth and nurturance and providing the source of our most exquisite delights As to the child so to the artist The mother takes the place of Nature in the life of the child, if she cannot fulfil his needs and provide the fount of spontaneous delight in his life she is not a true mother, the two functions are infact connected. If the mother cannot fulfil the child's needs neither can she become source of his joy. Such a link is also perceptible in Tagore's concept of education. A kind of relationship is imperative between Man and Nature which can enable the latter to not only supply our practical needs but nurture and cherish the child mind in us, the artist's vision in us and became an area of love and joy. Sisr Kumar Ghose in his paper '*Education in Utopia*' discusses at length of Tagore's ideals of education and the difference between the old Visva-Bharati and the new. Child, Nature, Tapovana. Rural Community, Aesthetics, Centre of Indian Culture, Eastern University, Visva-Bharati, what are these but a map of Rabindranath's creative mind, his humanistic syllabus of total education. The whole thing was finely tailored to his temperament. It was indeed the poem of his mind the epic of his lyric soul. Truth to tell, Santiniketan lived and died with Tagore.

Prema Nandakumar mentions that modern Indian has

not lacked seasoned educational messiahs-among others were Annie Besant, Malaviya. Subramania Bharati and J. Krishnamurti–But almost the first among them was Rabindranath Tagore. Their approaches might have differed in emphasis but their god was individual enlightenment and humanity And they generally based their educational theories firmly on India's ashram ideal, Dr. P.V. Rao recollects it was Tagore who declared that we needed a system of education in which emotion language and life shall be fairly combined... He was revolting against the educational system of the then British India He was revolting against a system that could only create slaves and destroy our very cultural roots.... Tagore however does not totally alienate his ideals of education from the rest of the world, though, he stresses on Indianisation. He consistently maintains that Universal brotherhood can be achieved only by a sound system of education. He admits that the western learning and science have done a great deal for mankind. But he strongly feels that without the aid of oriental culture the West fails to bring happiness to mankind. The West has need of the East and the East cannot divorce itself from the West."

The third session on 30 August, 1986 was chaired by Prof. Shiv Mangal Singh 'Suman' The papers on the theme Rabindranath Tagore and Literature : All Pervasive Excellence of Many splendoured Genius were contributed by two scholars namely Naresh Guha and S. Guptan Nair, (while Prof. Attar Singh spoke on the occasion). The Papers were :–

Guha, Naresh Rabindranath Tagore : the last phase of his poetry.

Guptan Nair, S. Tagorean synthesis.

Prof. Naresh Guha while discussing the last phase of

Tagore's poetry rightly states that even when they live long, creative men rarely remain vigorously active after they reach seventy Rabindranath was among those few extraordinary human beings who did. His creative energy defined the inevitable infirmity of age, and annexed untried areas of artistic expression like painting for instance. During the concluding years of his long life, he wrote few serious prose, about 527 poems in 9 volumes till 1937. Another 271 poems had been added which filled another eleven volumes, including one that was posthumous. But regarding the quality of this final crop, Prof. Guha attempts to give a brief summary of articles published in the first seven volume of '*Kavita*' the first all poetry Bengali journal all written by Buddhadeb Bose and also spoke about his lecture delivered at the University of Calcutta. According to Bose, his poetic faith and poetic vision remained unchanged after Gitanjali But Abu Sayed Ayyub opposed this view and opined that those poems written during the last decade of the poet's life, not only superior in merit, but also express a new tragic vision of life and the world which signified a clear rejection of his earlier faith and confidence in human destiny. Prof. Naresh Guha suggest that the poems of the last decade of Tagore be read alongwith other poems written before to reach a composite view. Prof. S. Guptan Nair in his *'Tagorean synthesis'* talks about the story of those spontaneous excitement which his Gitanjali poems with its subtle imagery and mastery of cadence had created. He feels that the present generation today considers them as wooly and wordly stuff. And then, there is on it, the label of mysticism, quite and unfashionable thing in modern literary circle. It was actually not Tagore but the western critics who made such a furore over his so-called mysticism. The initial worshipful approach to Gitanjali. Though it thrilled Tagore in the beginning began to annoy him afterwards "Oh, they are trying to find mysticism in all my poems" The poet is said to have exclaimed. Prof. Guptan Nair regrets that some people find it difficult to reconcile his great concern for the communication with the infinite. But we know that Tagore did combine the worldly and the other—worldly in the most natural way. He added "Tagore was poet who found the real joy of creation whether it was poetry that he created or a school for boys or a village reconstruction centre, if was the repetition of the eternal lila of the creator. This was the synthesis that this many splendoured genius achieved."

The Fourth session on *'Rabindranath Tagore in Translation : Awaiting New Translators'* was held on 30 August 1986. This concluding session was chaired by Prof. Umashandar Joshi. Prof. Harbhanaj Singh spoke on the occasion, while the papers were contributed by the following writers :–

Bhattacharya, B.K. *Tagore the novelist*

Gurdatta, Pradhan, *Rabindranath Tagore in translation; awaiting new translators*

Shivani, Gaura Pant *Rabindranath aur anuvad* (In Hindi)

Dr. B.K. Bhattacharya in his paper *'Tagore the Novelist'* gives a critical insight into his novel 'Ghare Baire' He mentions about Tagore the poet is so wellknown that Tagore the fiction-writer is often forgotten. Dr. Bhattacharya deals with Tagore's narrative style and creative vision. He says this novel perhaps set the trend of writing a psychological novel. Written in 1916, it also has a historical value with some sociological lesson for us. The novel refers to the communal propaganda and riots. His idea of secularism is well represented here what probably intrigued Tagore was the gradual alienation of the Muslims and the down trodden from the Swadeshi movement : His ideas of economic development and eradication of pains is based on philanthropy freedom of the individual and voluntary involvement of the masses. This critique is meant to emphasise the nature of the rural environment that inhibits development of ideal human relationship, specially the man-woman relationship. Here the society merely provided the background for the development :"

Pradhan Gurudatta in his papers gives particular reference to Rabindranath Tagore's translations in Kannada and the need for new translations–i.e., Tagore awaiting new translators. He says Ravindra literature in Kannada makes astonishing revelations during the last sixty and odd years. But still his impressive literature have not been able to create an influence of lasting value, as seldom these Kannada renderings have been attempted with all seriousness, and from the primary source. Even Smt. Gaura Pant Shivani in her paper *Ravindranath aur anuvad'* in Hindi briefly survey Tagore's writings in Hindi, be it his poems, short-stories dramas or novels, that miss the elusive qualities of the originals. But for Target language readers such rendering are welcome none-the-less because even half a loaf is better than none, she quotes Srinivasa lyenger.

This seminar ended with the valedictory address made by Prof. Amlan Dutta.

(III) International Seminar to mark the 50th Death Anniversary of Rabindranath Tagore (1991)

At Indian International Centre, New Delhi, an International Seminar was organised from 7th to 9th August (1991) to commemorate the 50th death anniversary of Rabindranath Tagore. The three National Akademies in collaboration with Indian Council for Cultural Relations arranged the function. On display 'was an exhibition of

Tagore's paintings (prints) and cultural activities were held in the evening on each of the three days : on the seventh there was a programme of recitations of some of Tagore's poems followed by a recital of *Nutan Bouthan* by Sri Vasant Chowdhury, on the eight, in programme of Rabindra Sangeet by Sri Subinoy Roy and Smt. Suchitra Mitra : and on the ninth Calcutta's *Theatron* Group enacted Tagore's play. 'Bisarjan' at Shri Ram Centre, Safadar Hashmi Marg, New Delhi. Sahil Bandyopadhyay in his director's Note stated : Dharma to Rabindranath did not merely mean religious faith but a very process of 'man's becoming a man 'the search for humanness in a human being which seems to be the central theme of his play. It is for this reason that in an age of religious fanaticism and political opportunism Theatron' feels the urge of performing Bisarjan again and again. The cast and credit of this production was :–

Raghupati	:	Babu Dutta Roy
Gobindamanikya	:	Dabashis Royachoudhury
Nakshatraray	:	Ashoke Banerjee
Mantri	:	Chuni Dutta
Gunabati	:	Madhuchhanda Ghose
Jaysimha	:	Sumanta Mukherjee
Nayanray	:	Joy Sengupta
Chandpal	:	Dipak Mitra
Courtier	:	Sanjay Ghosh
Aparna	:	Arunita Roychoudhury
Dhruba	:	Somnath Dutta
Guards	:	Amit Karmakar
	:	Bikas Roy
	:	Raju Mandal

The People	:	Ashesh Choudhury
		Arun Dutta
		Ajay Sen
		Tapas Bhandari
		Nabendu Sengupta
		Bikas Roy
		Biswajit Mukherjee
		Raju Mandal
		Dipak Thakurta
		Susmita Mukherjee
		Shipra Dutta
		Sujita Dey
		Shekhar Biswas
		Somnath Datta

Credits

Light Design	:	Tapas Sen
(Operation)	:	Badal Das
Sets Design	:	Gautam Basu
(Construct)	:	Ashoke Banerjee
Music	:	Partha Sengupta
(Operation)	:	Sripati Das
Costume	:	Debashis Roychoudhury
Make up	:	Manik Hossain
Editing and Direction	:	Salil Bandyopadhyay

It is significant to mention here that it was on the advice of Dr. Shankar Dayal Sharma, Vice-President of India that for the first time in the history of the three National Akademies their Secretaries along with the Director-General, ICCR met under the Chairmanship of Dr. Man Mohan Singh, the then Chairman U.G.C., to plan in a concerted way a year long programme on Tagore. In keeping with the Indian sentiment of observingdeath anniversary it was decided to start the function on a solemn note with an International Seminar entitled *Tagore's Vision of India : Its Relevance Today Fifty years After the Poet's death.* The seminar began on Wednesday 7 August 1991 (16 Sravana 1913 'Saka') with rendering of a song which Tagore had specifically wanted to be sung for the first time after his death. In his welcome address, Secretary, Sahitya Akademi stated". It is true that a rekindling of interest in Tagore has taken place all over the world and if it is a little dimmed it is only because now in place of initial exuberance shown at the time of his receiving the Nobel Prize, the lovers of literature are more keen to understand him as a complete writer–a writer who is as relevant today as he was seventy-eight years ago in 1913. New there is a potential audience all over the world who would like to understand Tagore in his totality. At least people have begun to re-assess him not as a mystic poet but as a poet of the people, a dramatist of deep human understanding, a social thinker of great compassion and a universal man of profound vision. This new situation has prompted us to pick out some important themes for discussion in this seminar, such as Tagore's idea of Indian history, his understanding of Indian plurality and unity, Tagore's vision and Modern India, Tagore and Indian Freedom struggle and Translating "Tagore".

He added that Tagore is an unending treasure for all of us, and it is essential that he be brought before the world for a better understanding of the common heritage of both East and West which we cherish so dearly. While inaugurating the International Seminar, the Chief Guest, Dr. Shankar Dayal Sharma presented an insightful paper on Tagore's work. He hoped that a wealth of ideas will emerge and will be critically evaluated in the course of the Seminar. Criticism and evaluation are necessary for a meaningful understanding of any great contribution. May I say that whenever I read Tagore and Whatever I read of him, even after critical scrutiny regarding the aesthetics or effect or plot or narration or logic, the impression that has remained with me has always been one of enjoyment and a reawakening or ennoblement of the heart. To me he is a poet Infact this seminar is devoted more to Tagore's thoughts on various seminal issues and not so much to his creative works. Yet I prefer to talk about Tagore the artist rather than about Tagore the thinker because of the simple reason that his thoughts cannot be properly be evaluated without reference to his poetry and music and painting" The inaugural speech was following by the addresses by the Heads of the three Akademies Sri Girish Karnad, Chairman of the Sangeet Natak Akademi, dealt with Tagore plays and regretted that it was an area still lying on the periphery. They require, he said, a greater exploration Sri Ram Niwas Mirdha. Chàirman Lalit Kala Akademi in his address, referred to Tagore as a non-conformist who did not follow the beaten track. Dr. Birendra Kumar Bhattacharya, President of the Sahitya Akademi in his Presidential address dwelt on Tagore's views on Indian history which provide the keys to understanding his view on other topics of the Seminar namely Indian plurality and unity, Indian freedom movement, his vision of India and universal man and also on Ancient Indian literature as a whole. The Indian historians also may find his views interesting because at a time when the imperialist historians presented a distorted picture of Indian history, Tagore countered it by offering his own picture. It was a picture depicted mainly on the basis of ethno cultural data" Again to Quote Dr. Bhattacharya. "He was no narrow nationalist and believed that *Swaraj* in India should be enjoyed equally by all ethnic and religious groups. He was against domination of one group by another and pleaded for equal and just development of different segments of Indian society. He conceived India as *mahajati,* federation by subnational groups comprising the nation" Dr. Birendra Kumar Bhattacharya made significant and scholarly observations on Tagore's vision of modern India. As a poet with a vision of life, Rabindranath gained deep in sigth into history of Indian. He spoke briefly about Tagore's essays on the history of India, his views on *Swaraj,* freedom struggle patriotism imperialist exploitation narrow nationalism and so on and finally gave a passing look at Tagore's vision of universal man. In his keynote address. Prof. Amlan Dutta, former Vice-Chancellor of Visva Bharati and an eminent economist and thinker stressed that Tagore's practical relevance has never been greater than at this juncture of history.

Dr. L.M. Singhvi, India's High Commissioner to U.K. and a well known jurist who was present on the occasion informed how he retrieved a very important Tagore manuscript 'Sarodotsava', some original Gitanjali songs, letters etc (all comprising of 460 pages) from a London auction house.

Prof. Gadgil, Vice-President, Sahitya Akademi presented the vote of thanks. As stated before, the themes taken up for discussion were :–

1. *Tagore's Idea of Indian History*;
2. *Tagore and the Indian Freedom Struggle*;
3. *Tagore's Vision and Modern India*;
4. *Tagore's Understanding of Indian Plurality and Unity*; and
5. *And Translating Tagore*

In the course of the Seminar eminent scholars and writers read-out papers. Each paper was followed by discussions. The various sessions were chaired by Prof. Gangadhar Gadgil, Dr. Ravinder Kumar, Prof. P.C. Joshi and Prof. Harbhajan Singh.

Among those who read papers were :–

Gadgil, Gangadhar	:	Tagore's Interpretation of Indian History
Bhattacharya, Malini	:	Tagore's Understanding of Indian Plurality and Unity (synopsis)
Das, Manoj	:	-do-
Detha, Vijayadan	:	Rabindranath kechintan main Bharat ki 'Vividhta' aur 'Ekta' ka Sandharbha "Mahamilan"
Ghosh, Surjit	:	Tagore's Understanding of Indian Plurality & Unity
Kim Yang-Shik	:	Tagore's vision in Modern Korean poetry
Kurup, O.N.V.	:	Tagore and Indian Freedom Struggle
Morimoto] Tatsuo	:	Tagore and the Awakening of Indian Nationalism in 19th century Bengal
Mukhopadhay, Subhash	:	Tagore's Vision of Indian History : Looking Back for a Forward Move
Namvar Singh	:	Tagore and Indian Freedom Struggle : the Current of History and the Flash of

		Lightning Tagore's view of Indian History.(English and Hindi)
Naravane, Vishwanath	:	Tagore's Vision and Modern India
Patel, Bholabhai	:	-do-
Radice, William	:	Translating Tagore
Trivedi, Harish	:	Nation, Race and Individuals : Tagore and his Englishmen
Verma, Shivendra K.	:	Your Mother Tongue is Your Best Tongue
Wa Bai-hui	:	Gurudeva Ever Lives in Our Heart

Gangadhar Gadgil in his paper *'Tagore's interpretation of Indian history'* mentions that Tagore rejects the view that history is primarily the record of states, wars, conquests, dynastic intrigues, interstate quarrels etc. To him history is a record of social life in all its dimensions and above all of the operative ideas that give direction to social processes. Thus is a view which now almost universally accepted. Gadgil further State that Tagore concedes that in Europe, if a king is defeated, the whole country is brought to the brink of destruction. Society loses its vitality, discipline and moving force. That is why in Europe politics is taken so seriously and history is preoccupied with the rise and fall of states.... Tagore pointed out that in Indian history society was more important that the state. Hindu political thinkers considered the state to be a necessary institution. But in India dharma sutras have a greater sanctity than the statras book or edicts of Kings.... Thus the governing principle of Indian social and Indian history has been to promote unity in the midst of diversity. India has tried to achieve this through social regulation of difference on the one hand and spiritual recognition of unity on the other.

Malini Bhattacharya in her short but interesting paper discusses Tagore's Understanding of Indian Plurality and Unity. She opines that no study of Rabindranath-texts today, fifty years after his death, can proceed without a consideration of their contextually. The concept of India or 'Bharatvarsha' as it is mostly called in the Rabindranath texts, appears embedded within a complex texture of responses to successive historical phases, as for example, the nascent national consciousness in Brahmo social reform movements of the 1880s. The rising tide of the Swadeshi struggle in the first decade of the 20th century and the gradually exposed aggressiveness of Western 'nationalism' particularly in the two world wars. It is also an interesting feature of the Rabindranath-texts that chronologically speaking, they start with an exphasis on the 'unity' of India and it is in subsequent phases of the discourse, that this is problematised through the projection of the concept of 'plurality'.

She exemplify by taking up the novel *Gora,* one of Rabindranath's best and most ambitious works in the genre as a focul point of the discourse, throwing light both on earlier and later phase in it... Gora comes in the wake of the first flush of enthusiasm for the 'Swadeshi' movement. This had been triggered off by Curzon's decision to redistribute the territories of the State of Bengal in accordance with the composition, in terms of Hindus and Muslims, of the population in the different districts.

The agitation against this Government order, known as 'Banga-bhanga andolan' helped to emphasize the 'unity' of Bengalis, and implicitly constructed the notion of an

Indian 'unity' threatened by foreign rulers. Rabindranath's initial ardour and subsequent questioning regarding this construct of Indian unity also become evident in the text of *Gora.* These questions would take a sharper form in *Chaturanga* and *Ghare-Baire* what constitutes our interest in the Rabindranath-texts, is that his perception of Indian 'unity' is not seamless and monolithic, but contains conceptual devises which may be used fordisrupting and dismantling this perception through an indication of its historical limits. This is the point at which the notion of 'plurality' appears. Thus in *Gora,* the eponymic hero's 'Hindu' perception of 'Bharatvarsha' is continually called to question and the notion of 'unity' inhering in it disrupted through a series of discursive counterpoints culminating in the discovery of the truth regarding the hero's birth... Plurality which for Rabindranath is aesthetically viable is made admissible in the lives of the people. And at this point, we can trace the source of this approach to *Gora* again, where *Gora* with the discovery of his identity, is reconciled through his mother with the low caste women who had been his nurse and whom he had subsequently not been able to accept. Manoj Das in his paper on the same theme pointed out that Tagore earned his right to proclaim the basic unity at the root of India's cultural and social plurality through an identity with the phenomenon and a soul-realisation of it and not through an intellectual conviction. His childhood experiences with nature and men reinforced this faith in him. While several of his poems bear the stamp of this realisation, in his series of essays entitled *Sadhana* and his Hibbert Lectures entitled *The Religion of Man,* he made the idea explicit through a smooth combination of rational and suprarational observations. The Upanishads, of course, were the mainstay of his philosophy, but his understanding of them was not academic or conventional but highly creative, as is evident from his interpretation of an Upanishadic statement. Manoj Das further observes :

> Tagore was a believer in man's future, but not in an emotional way. While hailing the sublime tradition of plurality in ancient India, he decried its perversion and took his countrymen to task for the situation through a powerful poem entitled *Apamanita.* At the same time he offered prayers to the Divine to awaken the sense of right values in the hearts of his countrymen. His last poem in *Gitanjali* is a moving description of his journey into the One-from which the multiple manifestation was possible.

Vijaydan Detha, the veteran Rajasthani writer also dealt with Tagore's understanding of Indian plurality and unity in his paper in Hindi entitled *'Rabindranath ke chintan mein Bharat ke vividhta aur ekta ka sandarbh 'Mahamilan'.*

Surajit Ghosh mentioned that Tagore's testament for posterity is collected in his *'Atma Parichay',* where in all the essays Tagore connected himself with multinational layers. *Atma Parichay* ends in a mantra which says about relatedness with the many. Tagore accepts the concept that the enlighten is one who is related with plural forces. This is Tagore's world vision and poetic vision too. His world vision can again be converted to his Indian vision as he has seen world in India, in India's unity in Diversity... Where in National Anthem or in Bharattirtha he not only united the whole country but also made the *Bhirgatas* a part of India—they came from outside, and no longer remained as foreigners (Refer-*Hethay Arya, Hetha Anarya*). This is how the plural forces are united in one string in India and Tagore's Nationalism transcends to *Viswamanabata.* Surajit Ghosh went further to explain that Tagore's revelation of Bharatatma was not only painted in his writings, it was translated in his performances, external work field and he tried to take it to the whole world during his tours over the world.

Kim Yang-Shik in his paper *'Tagore's Vision in Modern Korean Poetry'* informs us that during Tagore's 3rd visit to Japan in 1929, he was asked to visit Korea by some of the Korean patriotic youths in Tokyo at that time, he could not pay a visit to Korea. Instead, he left the following four line poem on Korea...

"In the golden age of Asia
Korea was one of its lamp-bearers
And that lamp is waiting to be lighted once again
For the illumination of the East."

He had sympathized with the revolt as human being. What had been expressed on the surface might have seemed weak, but deep in his heart there lay a fierce anger. The injustice of the world and society was exceedingly great. O.N.V. Kurup in his paper entitled *'Tagore and Indian Freedom Struggle'* briefly discusses 'Rabindranath's role in the struggle for independence his participation in the first session of the Indian National Congress in 1886, prosecution of Bal Gangadhara Tilak in 1877 Partition of Bengal and some stray incidents, till in 1908 when he withdrew from politics and turned to rural reconstructions and to his creative pursuits. Kurup observes that Tagore fought throughout his life against intellectual slavery which according to him was more dangerous than political slavery. Though Tagore and Gandhiji represented the same national tradition, though they drank deep from the same sacred scriptures and though they had the same goal, an independent India. Gandhiji and Gurudev were different; their ways of life were totally different; the roles they played in Indian freedom struggle also were different.

Tatsuo Morimoto in the paper *'Tagore and the Awakening of Indian Nationalism in 19th Century Bengal'* comments that Gandhiji sowed a seed of non-violent revolution in the soil tilled by the plough of Tagore's ardent bu universal minded patriotism. Morimoto states that Tagore's voice of anger and indignation was not directed only to the British Government and its officials, because he resented all the injustices, tyrannies and exploitation by whomever done. Once, after a session of the early Indian National Congress held in Calcutta Taraknath Palit, a wealthy barrister of the Calcutta High Court, gave a dinner at his house to the political leaders assembled from the every parts of India on the occasion. According to Rathindranath Tagore, Poet's eldest son, although Tagore was reluctant to go to an English dinner, the host wished him insistently to attend to entertain the guests with a few songs. Then, "Father's resentment found voice in the words of the songs he composed :–

> *Do not ask me to sing, I pray you*
> *ask me not.*
> *Is this as mere matter of laugh and play,*
> *and of falsehood and deceptions."*
> *("On the Edges of Time")*

And yet, he appeared "in the midst of the anglicised dinners" in dhoti an chaddar as an indication of his protest itself. Then "there was an embarrassing hush, after which the party broke up", continues the writer. It was after a quarter century when Gandhiji appeared on the political scene of India that "The whole look of the Congress changed : European chothes vanished and soon only khadi was to be seen (from J. Nehru : "*An Autobiography*"). Thus Tagore was a John, the Baptist, "waiting for the Mahatma" in the sacred drama of Indian Independence.

Subhas Mukhopadhyay, in his essay titled *'Tagore visionof Indian history : looking back for a forward move'* mentions about the most distinctive trait of Indian history and civilization which according to Tagore, is not, political but principally social and cultural. Indian history and culture were not state oriented; rather, they sprouted from multifold self regulating local societies, known as 'Swadeshi Samaj'. From time immemorial, successive waves of peoples of diverse cultures and ways of life have come and struck root in India. Through an unceasing process of integration and assimilation, we have achieved unity in diversity... Tagore called Indian the sea-shore of great humanity where numerous people coming form different directions have merged into a single body. Adjustment, harmony and synthesis-these have been the greatest challenges his paper both in English and in Hindi entitled *'Tagore and Indian freedom struggle the current of history and the flash of lightning : Tagore's view of Indian history'* and *Bharat ke bare mein Rabindranath ki dristi, bartaman sandarbh mein uski prasangikata : itihas ki dhara aur vidyucchhata; Rabindranath ki dristi mein Bharat ka itihas*' respectively points out that Tagore raised his voice against nationalism at a time when national awakening was at its peak. This required no ordinary courage. Putting up with popular opprobrium, the poet in him went on writing patriotic song such as *'Bharata-Tirtha'* on the one hand and pointing out the limitations of nationalism through a novel like *Ghara Baire* on the other hand. A consequence of this was Tagore's confrontation with the Father of the Nation, Mahatma Gandhi over the issue of A Non-cooperation whose historical document is the essay *"Satyer Ahvan"* (The Call of the Truth, 1921)"

Vishwanath Narayane in the in the paper *'Tagore's vision and modern India'* observes :

In *Jana gana mana* we have a succession of images

of India's past and her present. I know of no other national as them in which such exquisite music and poetry are blended with so much wisdom and deep insight into the country's past. I cannot think of any other poet whose partiotism has been expressed with such universal love. In these few stanzas Tagore has summed up entire cultural history of India. He has captured the excitement and the drama of centuries, the mingling of faiths, the fusion of races, the subtle unity that runs through the diversity of language and ritual climate and landscape."

Bholabhai Patel in his paper titled *'Tagore's vision and modern India'* touches upon some aspects of vast and varied image of India which we find in Tagore's creative writings. He chose to discuss more paradoxical aspects of Tagore's response to emergent narrow Indian Nationalism and his subsequent turning to internationalism during the crucial phase of last decade of 19th century and the first decade of 20th century William Radice in *'Translating Tagore'* states the great self-discipline is needed if one is to be a faithful interpreter and not fall into the temptation of 'improving' one's original and furnishes Ten Rules for translating Tagore (1986)

1. The work must be done slowly
2. The translations must be accurate
3. The translations must be accompanied by explanation
4. Tagore's poetry should be translated into poetry
5. Translation should have depth
6. The translator must be selective
7. The translation must have a unifying quality of rhythm.
8. The translation must have sympathy

9. The translation should seem new
10. The work of translation should be done with love.

Harish Trivedi in *'Nation' race and individuals : Tagore and his English men'* writes that Tagore's uncompromizing internationalism was accommodated within nationalism and even sought to be appropriated for it by enlightened nationalists such as Gandhi and Nehru. "Gurudev himself is international because he is truly national." Gandhi declared following his visit to Visva Bharati in 1940, while Nehru had in a tribute in 1931 said that "*Tagore has given our nationalism the outlook of internationalism and has enriched it.*" It is through such compelling inclusive representation that Tagore, with all his unyielding anti-nationalism, is yet popularly (and ironically) seen as one of the trinity of India's great national and nationalist-leaders of this century, together with Gandhi and Nehru themselves. Shivendra Kumar Verma's paper entitled *'Your mother tongue is your best tongue'* dealt with Tagore's perception of the role of the mother tongue in education. Here he discusses the role of language and problems in a multilingual setting and states that Tagore felt the best language of education for human learner is the language of his family and surroundings his mother tongue or effective 'first language' the best way of understanding the universe around us and of expressing our experiences was in terms of the mother tongue.

According to Tagore, it was the suppression of the mother tongue that led to education anaemia in Ireland. Tagore was not opposed to the teaching and learning of English, but it can and should be used as a second window on the expanding universe around us.

Wu Bai-hui's paper *"Gurudeva ever lives in our hearts"* refers to Gurudeva's Vedantic Vision, Truth,

Brahma, Para-Brahma etc. and tries to derive an illustratiye formula from Tagore's metaphysical vision :–

(a) infinity

(b) finitude

(c) unity of truth (in one's self)

This formula is of great significance in the first place, it tells that there exist, between the two aspects of Truth, both the contradiction and the unity, the former second to the latter; and that the unity of Truth must be sought in the realm of spirit, the Brahma-loka where dwells the para-Brahma, and where the individual self could be in touch with Supreme Person.

At the end, Wu Bai hui states "It is evident that the most advanced sciences and technologies of the contemporary world has been bestowing on the modern man the ability and capacity of acquiring mastery over nature, exuberant material wealth and all sorts of untodaticus comforts and luxuries. But, it is a great pity that they are not the spiritual omniscience after all, they fail miserably to salvage him from the spiritual "*duhkha-samudra*" or the spiritual suicide as Gurudeva calls. One may asks, "It there no way out for him spiritually then?" My answer is positive and optimistic, for we are fortunately the beneficiaries of Gurudeva's divine wisdom which is always inspiring us with knowledge and courage and Gurudeva's sacred teachings, being the invaluable cultural heritage not only of India, but of the world also, is the spiritual amrta-elixir vitae by which to relieve, with efficacy, the spiritual crisis that is threatening our contemporary civilization."

(IV) Seminars on Gora (1993)

In 1993, the Sahitya Akademi adopted a new scheme to discuss important classics and seek their relevance today.

The programme is in the form of a series of discussions on select Indian classics alone. The first classic chosen was Rabindranath Tagore's *'Gora'*.

On 21 April 1993, the first seminar in the series was held at Mumbai. This one-day literary forum seminar was attended by eminent writers, critics and intellectuals of the metropolis. Sri Ramchandra Sarkar and Sri Ramji Tiwari led the discussions as Sri Vijay Tendulkar, noted Marathi playwright, who was also to take part in the discussion could not attend. The session as chaired by Dr. Suresh Dalal. During the course of discussion, Sri Suresh Dalal referred to *Gora* as a timeless classic which has kept up the relevance. He stated, given a choice, he would re-name the book 'Anandamoyee'.

Dr. Ramji Tiwari of Pune Vidyapith said that the chief message of Gora is that humanity is the greatest religion. It was not significant whether Gora was a Hindu or a Brahmin by birth. What is significant is he was an Indian.

Sri Ramchandra Sarkar said that reading the novel was a unique experience for him and he discussed some aspects of the novel, including its relecanve today. The seminar ended with an interesting question answer session.

The venue of the nest seminar on Gora was New Delhi that was held on 30 April 1993 Prof. U.R. Anantha Murthy chaired the session. Dr. Harish Trivedi and Dr. Sisir Kumar Das of the University of Delhi and Dr. Namwar Singh, wellknown Hindi critic, led the discussions.

Prof. Anantha Murthy said that *Gora* was a "fundamental novel." Itt is amazing, he added, that Rabindranath addressed himself to such profound questions as is found in the novel. A lyrical writer can think of India as a nation but a novelist cannot, but Tagore was both and hence we have novel like *Gora.* It is in this novel that we have for

Seminar on Gora in Mumbai

Seminar on Gora in Hampi

(Prof. U. R. Anantha Murthy delivering his address)

the first time a picture of the Indian village and also the conflict of attitudes tradition and modernity, purity and impurity, past and present, and East and West.

Dr. Harish Trivedi mentions that *Gora* is vast both in scope and treatment and referred to its theme as "grand". He points out that the novel raised a national agenda then and raises one now.

Dr. Sisir Kumar Das mentions that the narrator reminds the reader of particular date 1857. *Gora* was born that year and without Tagore's intending to write a historical novel, it became one, though it has no historical characters as such. Dr. Das says that it in evident from the novel that Tagore rejected formal Hinduism and looked back into the folk sources of religion Infact, Tagore constitutes his own view of Hinduism which is not readily accepted.

Lastly, Dr. Namwar Singh spoke on the occasion. He said that the great test of a secular person is during marriage and death. It is an these two occasions that religion comes in the way, however modern or open-minded he may be. The universal truth has been admirably depicted in *Gora.*

The presentations were followed by fruitful discussions and lively debates among writers, critics, intellectuals of the Delhi circle.

Finally on 19 June 1993, the last seminar on *Gora* was organised at Hampi under the joint venture of the Sahitya Akademi and the Kannada University. The seminar was inaugurated by Prof. U.R. Anantha Murthy, President, Sahitya Akademi in his inaugural speech he said the novel *Gora,* has depicted the limitations, the ideals and the in build tolerance of Hinduism. Its relevance in the present socio-political context in India can hardly be over emphasised.

Dr. Shanthinath Desai, former Vice-Chancellor,

Kuvempu University, and Sri Anis Ul Haq, Director, were the chief guests. Dr. Desai stated that Tagore, in this novel, examines the relationship between human beings and the religions Sri Anis Ul Haq felt the need to discuss Indian writings more than foreign works.

This function was then presided over by Dr. Chandrasekhar Kambar, Vice-Chancellor of Kannada University, and also an outstanding poet and play with.

In his address, Dr. Kambar observed that the relationship between different languages should be meaningful. He also talked about the dangers of colonialism.

Dr. K.V. Narayana, Registrar of the University, welcomed the guests. Sri C. Srinivasa Raju, proposed a vote of thanks.

The First Session of the Seminar was presided over by Sri Anis Ul Haq Prof. K.D. Kurtkoti, Prof. K.R. Nagaraj and Prof. G.H. Nayak presented their papers on *"Gora-Bases of Study"*. The scholars discussed the following topics *Gora Indian Literature, 'Gora in the Background of Colonialism'* and *'The concept of Hinduism and Gora'*.

The presentation were followed by thought provoking discussions. The Second Session was chaired by Dr. Sisir Kumar Das who spoke on some aspects of Tagore's literary outputs. Prof. Anantha Murthy, Dr. Desai and Dr. Kambar took part in this session and responded to the novel in the background of their creative experience.

The Seminar was attended by several distinguished scholars, critics, intellectuals, journalist, painters, performing artists and literary fraternity of Karanataka Sri P.R. Tippeswamy, President, Karanataka Lalita Kala Akademi, Sri Mudenooru Sanganna, folklorist, Smt. Gangubai Hangal, the renowned Hindustani vocalist, Prof. R.M. Hadapad, painter, Dr. Besagarahalli Ramanna, short-story writer, Smt.

Sarah Abookbacker, novelist, Sri Chennaveera Kanavi, poet, Sri M.H. Krishnaiah, scholar and art critic, Sri. T.P. Ashok, critic, Dr. Basavaraj Mallashetty, scholar to name some.

Apart from Seminars, it was it was in the year 1967 that the Akademi ventured to start a Literary Forum at its Head Office in New Delhi. This kind of programmes were later introduced in its regional offices at Madras, Calcutta and Bombay.

To provide a nucleus for literary discussions and exchange of views among local writers and visiting litteratures, the Sahitya Akademi arranges periodical sessions of its Informal Literary Forum every years. Besides New Delhi, for the benefit of local litterateurs, the Regional offices of the Akademi also organises such literary programmes every year.

Given below are the particulars of the Tagore programmes arranged on these occasions : On 13th May 1973, Dr. B. Gopala Reddi gave an extensive lecture on the topic *'Some Thought on Rabindranath Tagore'* at Madras.

On 3 May 1977, Dr. B. Gopala Reddi, President, Andhra Pradesh Sahitya Akademi again spoke on Rabindranath Tagore and read Telugu translation of some of the poems by Tagore in a Literary Forum meeting held at Madras.

Dr. Amiya Chakarvarti, Visiting Fellow, Visva Bharati, gave a talk on *'Rabindranath and contemporary World Poets'* in a meeting of the Literary Forum held on 5 October 1977 at Calcutta.

On May 5, 1980, a literary programme was organised by the Regional Office at Madras under the Chairmanship of Sri P. Padmaraju, Dr. B. Gopala Reddi spoke on the many-sided personality of Tagore.

On 3 January 1986, the Sahitya Akademi organised an informal literary gathering in Calcutta in which Mr. William Radice, translator of Tagore poems, addressed a meeting at the Centre for Studies in Social Sciences. Distinguished writers and scholars participated.

On 10th February, 1990 Sri Sombhu Mitra eminent playwright and theatre personality, gave an absorbing talk on the modes of recitation, drawing wherever appropriate from his own theatrical experiences. He recited poems from Tagore and Jibanananda and extracts from his own play 'Chand Banikar Pala' to a large gathering of admirers.

From 7th to 9th August 1991, Sahitya Akademi's Regional Office at Calcutta organised talks on *'Tagore's Heine'* and *'Goethe and Tagore'*. Talk on "Tagore's Heine" and "Goethe and Tagore" To commemorate the 50th death anniversary of Rabindranath Tagore, Sahitya Akademi and Max Mueller Bhavan, Calcutta jointly organised these two lectures by Prof. Alokeranjan Dasgupta, Professor in the Department of Neo-Indology at the Heidelburg University, Germany. Sri S.V. Raman and Sri Ramkumar Mukhopadhyay welcomed the gathering on behalf of the Max Mueller Bhawan and Sahitya Akademi respectively. Dr. Dasgupta, in his first lecture, spoke on Tagore's translation of nine selected poems of Heine from German and attempted a semiological and phonological comparison between the original and the translated version. His second lecture was a study of *Sonar Tari* (The Golden Boat) in the perspective of the Popular Goethian maxim, "Entbehern sollst du, sollst entbehren/ thou must do without, must do without", which Tagore himself had quoted on the title page of his manuscript of the above book. The lectures were followed by a slide show entitled *Prometheus* directed by Sri Durgasankar Ghosh and Prof. Dasgupta, with relevant scenic readings by '*Sangbarta*'.

Sahitya Akademi and Max Mueller Bhavan, Calcutta

organised a series of three lectures by Dr. William Radice and Dr. Martin Kaempchen on 4, 5 and 6 September, 1991 on the occasion of Tagore's 50th Death Anniversary. It dealt with *'Tagore's significance today, 'Understanding Tagore's Short Stories'* and *'A Public Discussion on Translating Tagore into European Languages'*

Eminent Tagore scholars Prof. Amaln Dutta, Prof. Sibnarayan Ray, Dr. Ananda Lal and others were among those present in the audience.

Speaking on 'Tagore's Significance Today' Dr. Radice, Lecturer at the School of Oriental and African Studies, University of London, and the Language Supervisor for BBC's Bengali Service, asserted that Tagore's anti-materialism, educational ideals, his support for the emancipation of women, and his interpretation of the spiritual-all will emerge, if they are not already emerging as extremely significant for contemporary civilization. On the next day, Dr. Radice spoke on 'Understanding Tagore's Short Stories'. Analysing Tagore's celebrated short-story '*Thakurada*' during the course of it, he showed how there is in Tagore a tension between, a longing to enter the human world of happiness and sadness, meeting and parting, and a longing to rove freely in a world of unfettered beauty' (Pramathanath Bishi). The former mainly finds expression in the stories, the latter in the poems.

On the last day, there was a lively public discussion between Dr. Radice and Dr. Martin Kaempchen, a scholar of German literature who is presently doing research in Bengali at Santiniketan. Professor Sukanta Choudhuri conducted the session. Two poems of Tagore along with their German translations were also read out and the discussion hovered around the translability of subtle points of nuances and deviations. Again from 3rd to 5th, 10th to

12th and 16th to 17th December, Talks on Rabindranath Tagore and Germany (Lecture Series) were organised at Calcutta.

Another activity of the Akademi '*Literary Workshops*' started in the year 1976 where the writers ensemble and practise their art in the company of fellow-writers, discuss practical problems and exchanged views and experience.

On 23 November 1991, a Workshop in '*Translating Tagore in European Languages*' was also organised by the Calcutta Regional Office.

Apart from Seminars, Literary Forum Meetings and Workshops, Akademi takes up many more programmes of diverse nature. In '*Meet the Author*', a distinguished writer is invited to speak on this life and works, '*Men and Books*' in which eminent persons from interdisciplinary areas are invited to give lectures, '*Through My Window*' in which a writer of eminence presents his impression on the life and works. Likewise it has new literary programmes like *Kavisandhi, Kathasandhi, Loka : The Many voices, Asmita* and so on.

On 3 September 1991 at Sisir Mancha, Calcutta, the Sahitya Akademi organized its second '*Men and Books*' function wherein the eminent Rabindra Sangeet exponent, Smt. Suchitra Mitra was invited to speak on the occassion. In the courses of her interesting talk, Smt. Mitra described her life at Santiniketan, where as a student she had an opportunity to study the works of Tagore.

6
EXHIBITIONS

To hold literary exhibition is an important function of the Sahitya Akademi and is succinctly mentioned in its constitution (As embodied in the Government of India, Ministry of Education Resolution No. F 6-4/51 G-2 (A) dated the 15th December, 1952 and as amended from time to time).

Sahitya Akademi organizes and participates in literary exhibitions in various way. It could be a book exhibition as part of its sales promotional campaigns or a Biobibliographical exhibition on a litterature reflecting his life and work or an exhibition one witness during its Annual Festival of Letters, when the event begins customarily with the inauguration of an exhibition highlighting its activities and achievements over the year. A Collage of Newspaper reviews and photographs taken during various programmes of the previous year, a set of Akademi Award-winning books for that year and some of Akademi's recent publications are put on view.

It may be recalled that on the occasion of the Unesco General Conference in the winter of 1956, for the first time, the Sahitya Akademi participated in a major Exhibition of Indian Literature, in which books and important manuscripts in all the languages of India were exhibited. There was a separate section of book, in English written on or about India by Indian and foreign writers. A pioneer attempt, the exhibition was much appreciated by lovers of books. Since then, the Akademi is organizing numerous book exhibitions at various levels all over India.

Just before the head office of the Sahitya Akademi shifted from hutment's in Connaught Place to its new premises in the newly built Rabindra Bhawan at the end of November 1961, its adjacent Exhibition Hall of the Lalit Kala Akademi had already been inaugurated on the Tagore's Centenary date, 8th May 1961.

On this great cultural event, an exhibition of Rabindranath Tagore's life and works was inaugurated by the President of India.

As part of the world-wide celebration of the Birth Centenary, the Sahitya Akademi had also undertaken or participated in a series of book exhibitions during the year 1961. Some of these are

1. Exhibition of Rabindranath Tagore's works arranged by the Readers service, 81 Forbes Street, Bombay1
2. Exhibition of Tagore literature arranged by the Rabindra Satabarshik Utsav Samity, New Delhi-3
3. 'Tagore in India and Abroad' Exhibition organised at Madras by the Ministry for Scientific Research and Cultural Affairs (participated by the Regional Office, Madras)
4. Tagore exhibition organized by Tagore Centenary Peace Festival All India Committee, Calcutta (Participation by the Regional Office, Calcutta)

During the years 1963, the Akademi participated in the 'Tagore Books Exhibition', held by the Jamia Millia, Jamia Nagar, New Delhi. In May 1974, at Calcutta, during Kavi Paksha or Tagore Fortnight by the Tagore Research Institute, the Regional Office, Calcutta participated in a book-Exhibition. Again from 16th to 23rd July 1974 at

Calcutta, on the occasion of the Golden Jubilee of Visva Bharati Publication Department, the Akademi took part in it.

In a week-long book exhibition from 21 st October to 27th October 1976 at Shantiniketan during the 'Paus Mela' celebrations, Sahitya Akademi Regional Office put on display its own publications.

To celebrate the 125th birth anniversary, Akademi organised a book exhibition on 29 and 30 August 1986 at New Delhi.

It also participated in the book exhibition organised by the Tagore Society, Jamshedpur from 13th to 22 September 1987.

Again from 11 to 19 November 1989, Sahitya Akademi took part in a book fair organized by the Tagore Society at Jamshedpur.

From 8th to 15th August 1991, the Sahitya Akademi joined 'the Tagore Book Fair' at Calcutta, to commemorate Tagore's 50th Death Anniversary. An exhibition of News reports published in British Press from 1912-1941 entitled *'Rabindranath Tagore and the British Press'* was presented by Sahitya Akademi and the Tagore Centre UK from 22 23 December, 1993 at Lalit Kala Akademi Gallery. A publicity brochure published on the occasion stated"... Tagore's great works were unknown to the world outside Bengal until 1 12 when Tagore was fifty one. The poet's acquaintance with the West at that time was limited to two visits to London related to his academic career. His third visit to England in 1912 however turned out to be a major turning point in his life. The manuscript of his own English translations of his poems Tagore had carried to England during this visit was read and admired by W.B. Yeats, the great Irish poet, who found, those free verse compositions as exquisite in style as in thought. The publication of this work, *Gitanjali,* was immediately noticed by the Western literary world and on the merit of this single work Tagore was awarded the Nobel Prize for literature in 1913. His fame as a 'Seer from the East' took no time to reach Europe and America. Other works followed and were received with equal enthusiasm by the British public sphere. England kept up this interest in Tagore's life and works until the poet's death in 1941, though the response varied from elated adulation to evident disenchantment.

This exhibition is a faithful reflection of these changing moods of the British public as captured by the British print media of Tagore's time. The six hundred news items from the British dailies and the weeklies from the Tagore Centre, UK, from which the present selection has been made are sure to interest every Indian lover of letters. Arranged in chronological order with useful background materials, these rare exhibits recreate the image of Tagore as felt and known by the West of his time. They say as much about the poet as about the contemporary West : a retrospective articulation of two cultures meeting and assessing each other.

Detailed description of each Exhibit in given below :

Exhibit 1

Rabindranath Tagore was introduced to British poets and men of letters at a reception given in his honour at the Trocadero restaurant in London on July 10, 1912. The reception was arranged by the India Society with W.B. Yeats presiding. The report of this reception was published in *The Times (July* 13, 1912). This was the first report on Tagore which appeared in a British newspaper.

Exhibit 2

An editorial in *The Times* (July 16, 1912) on Tagore's address at the reception on July 10.

Exhibit 3

Maharani of Arakan—a play adapted by George Calderon from one of Tagore's short stories Daliya, was staged by the Indian Dramatic Society on July 30, 1912 at the Royal Albert Hall, London. Tagore was present. The report was published in *The Times (July* 31, 19132)

Exhibit 4

Facsimile of the cover and the frontispiece of the British *Gitanjali* published by the India Society in November 1912. The English *Gitanjali* is a collection of Tagore's own free verse recreation of 103 Bengali poems in English. Only 750 copies were printed. The Macmillan edition was published later in March 1913.

Exhibit 5

"... Few works of poetry published in English during recent years have made so deep an impression on the minds of thoughtful readers as this collection of translation from the Bengali, made by the author..." (Hibbert Journal). *Gitanjali* was accepted for its literary excellence by British readers. Reviews of *Gitanjali* published in *The Times Literary Supplement* (November 7, 1912), *The Nation* (November 16, 1912) and in *The Manchester Guardian* (January 14, 1913) were exhibited here.

Exhibit 6

Tagore read his own translation of *Chitrangada on* May 9, 1913 in the presence of an exclusive audience at the Indian Dramatic Society (set up in May 1912). The exhibited report of the reading appeared in *The Westminster Gazette* (May 10, 1913). This drama was later published as *Chitra by* the India Society.

Exhibit 7

The play *Post-Office* (a translation of *Dakgar)* was first staged in Dublin by the professional group of Abbey Theatre in aid of St. Enda's College on May *17,* 1913. The report shown was published in *The Irish Times* (May 19, 1913).

Exhibit 8

An interview with Tagore by a special correspondent of *The Christian Commonwealth* published in May 21, 1913.

Exhibit 9

Between 19 May and 25 June, 1913 Tagore delivered six lectures (one in each week) under the auspices of the Quest Society (A Society devoted to the study of religion and philosophy) at Caxton Hall, London. Full reports of the opening (May 24, 1913) and the concluding (June 28, 1913) lectures, published in *The Inquirer,* were exhibited here.

Exhibit 10

A report of the lecture delivered at the Manchester College, Oxford on May 23 was published in *The Christian Commonwealth* (May 28, 1913). Subject of the lecture :— *Reali.sation in Love.*

Exhibit 11

The report of the reception given to Tagore by Indian students in Great Britain—*Times* (June 16, 1913).

Exhibit 12

Tagore's short *story-The Judge (Bicharak)* published in *The Nation* (July 5, 1913). This was Tagore's first publication in a British periodical.

Exhibit 13

Post-Office was again staged in London on 10 July, 1913 at the Court Theatre by the same Abbey Group which performed in Dublin. The present reports shown were taken from *The Era (July* 16, 1913) and *The Stage* (July 17, 1913).

Exhibit 14

Between July 1913 and April 1914 Tagore's poems regularly appeared in fortnightly intervals in *The Nation.* Some were shown here.

Exhibit 15

Macmillan published Tagore's second book of verse*The Gardener* in October 1913. Reviews appeared in several dailies. The present three reviews are taken from the *Daily Mail* (October 29, 1913). *The Daily News and Leader* (October 27, 1913) and *The Daily Telegraph* (November 14, 1913).

Exhibit 16

On November 14, 1913 the news of the award to Tagore of Nobel Prize for literature appeared in almost all British dailies. The reports taken from *The Daily Chronicle, The Daily Express* and *The Daily Mail.*

Exhibit 17

Tagore's biographical sketches appeared in several newspapers and journals following the news of the award. *The Everyman* (edited by Ernest Rhys) published a special issue on Rabindranath Tagore on November 14, 1913. The fascimile of the cover and the inside article were exhibited here.

Exhibit 18

The editorial in *The Manchester Guardian* (November 15, 1913).

Exhibit 19

A biographical sketch appeared in T.P.'s *Weekly* (November 21, 1913).

Exhibit 20

A photograph with a brief mention of the award was published in *The Sketch* (November 19, 19131).

Exhibit 21

The award of the Nobel Prize to an Asian poet evoked certain amount of discontent in the British public especially when Thomas Hardy and Anatole France were two strong contenders that year. Unfavourable criticisms appeared in some newspapers and journals. The select examples were published in *The Daily News* and *Leader* (November 14, 1913), *The New Age* (November 2, 1913) and in *The New Statesman* (December 27, 1913).

Exhibit 22

A satirical note from *Punch* (December 10, 191 11).

Exhibit 23

An interesting article to establish a link between the visit of Prince William of Sweden and the Novel Prize awarded to Tagore was published in *Truth* (December ?4. 1913).

Exhibit 24

Tagore's poems of the child-series—*The Crescent Moon*, was published in November 1913. The reviews of the book came out in *Pall Mall Gazette* (November 26, 1913) and *The Globe* (November 27, 1913).

Exhibit 25

A cartoon with a poem in '*The Westminster Gazett*, (December 31, 1931).

Exhibit 26

How do you pronounce Rabindranath Tagore? From *Evening Standard* and St. James's Gazette (January 5, 1914).

Exhibit 27

An article on Shantiniketan school by J. Ramsay Macdonald was published in *The Daily Chronicle* (January 2, 1914).

Exhibit 28

Photograph of the reception held at Shantiniketan after the Novel Prize award—*The Graphic* (January 17, 1914).

Exhibit 29

Chitra was published by the India Society in 1913 The review of *Chitra* displayed came out in *The Athenaeum*, (January 17, 1914).

Exhibit 30

London Chat-*The Daily Citizen*, (February 7, 1914)

Exhibit 31

A biographical sketch and works of Tagore published in *The Baptist Times* and *Freeman* (February 13, 1914).

Exhibit 32

Sadhana—a book of philosophical essays—mainly

incorporating lectures delivered in *England and* USA in *1912, was* published in December *1913.* Reviews of *Sadhana* appeared in *The Spectator* (February 14, 1914), *The Manchester Guardian* (October 6, 1914) and *The Globe* (December 22, 1913) were exhibited.

Exhibit 33

Reviews of *The Gardener, The Crescent Moon, Sadhana* and *Chitra* published in *The Times Literary Supplement* May 14, 1914).

Exhibit 34

The above translation in two consecutive issues of *The Christian Commonwealth* (February 25 and March 4, 1914).

Exhibit 35

A brief and critical account of Shantiniketan School published in *The Daily Telegraph* (February 26, 1914).

Exhibit 36

The King of the Dark Chamber—a translation of the Bengali drama *Raja-was* published in *1914.* The two *reviews* displayed were published in *The Globe* (June 15, 1914) and *The Manchester Guardian* (October 6, 1914).

Exhibit 37

Reviews of the *Cresent* Moon, *The King of the Dark Chamber* and *Chitra* in The Outlook (October, 3, 1914).

Exhibit 38

The play *Post Office*--a translation of *Darkghar*—which was staged at the Court Theatre. London, during the summer of 1913, was later published by Macmillan in July 1914.

The translation was done by Devabrath Mukerjea. The present review came out in *The Times Literary Supplement* (October 15, 1914).

Exhibit 39

Tagore's poems published in *The Times* (October 26, 1914) and January 28, 1916).

Exhibit 40

A poem on Tagore in *The Liver pool Daily Post* and *Mercury* (May 15, 1915).

Exhibit 41

Tagore was knighted on June 3, 1915. The news wa published in almost all dailies. The shown report was from *The Daily Mail* (June 3, 1915).

Exhibit 42

Rabindranath Tagore : A biographical study by Earnest Rhys was the biography of Tagore published (Macmillan 1915) in the West The book was reviewed in several journals including the *Spectator* (June 26, 1915).

Exhibit 43

One Hundred Poems of Kabir—a collection of Kabir's poems, translated by Tagore in collaboration with Evelyn Underhill, was published by the India Society in 1914. The review appeared in *The Tinges Literary Supplement* (August 5, 1915).

Exhibit 44

A report of Shantiniketan School published in *The Times, Education Supplement* (September 21, 1916).

Exhibit 45

Reviews of *Fruit Gathering and Hungry Stones and Other Stories* (former is a collection of poems and the latter is a collection of short stories : both published by Macmillan in 1916) appeared in *The Times Literary Supplement* (November 23, 1916).

Exhibit 46

Report of the addresses delivered by Tagore in Japan denouncing the Western *civilization-The Times* (January 2, 1917).

Exhibit 47

During his tour of Japan in 1916 the poet often wrote short epigrams on hand fans or on handkerchiefs at the request of his Japanese visitors. Later on these verses were published as *Stray Birds* by Macmillan. *A* revicw of *Stray Birds* was published in *The Christian Commonwealth* (May 9,1917).

Exhibit 48

Personality-a collection of lectures delivered during his tour in USA (in 1916-1917) was published in 1917. The review came out in *The Times Literary Supplement* (June 6, 1917).

Exhibit 49

My Reminiscence-A translation of Tagore's memoirs Jivansmriti by Surendranath Tagore-was published in 1917. The exhibited reviews were published in *The Times Literary Supple rnent* (August 9, 1917) and *The Nation* (August 25, 1917).

Exhibit 50

Nationalism— another collection of lectures delivered

during his tour in Japan and USA (in 1916-1917) was published in 1917. The exhibited reviews were from *The Times Literary Supplement* (August 13, 1917) and *The New Statesman* (September 15, 1917).

Exhibit 51

Mashi and other Stories—another collection of short stories was published in 1918. The review of the book appeared in *The Times Literary Supplement* (April 18, 1918).

Exhibit 52

Report on two short plays, Savitri and *The King and the Queen (Raja or Rani)*, staged by the Indian Art and Dramatic Society, published in *The Stage* (February 20, 1919).

Exhibit 53

Review of-*The Home and the World (Ghare Baire)* — published by Macmillan in 1919, appeared in The Times *Literary Supplement* (May 29, 1919).

Exhibit 54

On April 13, 1919 troops under General Dyer fired at unarmed civilians in a peaceful gathering at Jalianwala Bagh. The poet was deeply shocked at this mindless massacre by the imperialist Government and wrote a letter to the Viceroy, condemning the mass killing and renouncing his knighthood. News of the massacre was covered up by the British press for a considerable time. The poet's decision of renunciation of the knighthood was published inconspicuously in *The Times* (June 19. 1919). However, the entire text of the letter was published later in *The Manchester Guardian* (July 9, 1919).

Exhibit 55

A brief news of the refusal of revocation of the title of knightood was published in *The Tunes* (August 2, 1919).

Exhibit 56

Report on the two short plays Sacrifice *(Bisarjan)* and *Chitra* staged by the Indian Art and Dramatic Society published in *The Observer* (May 9, 1920).

Exhibit 57

On Tagore's vision of "a fellowship of man"—*The Times* (January 6, 1921).

Exhibit 58

Report published in *The Morning Post* (April 9, 1921) on the lecture addressed at the Indian Students' Hostel, Subject—Meeting of *the East and the West.*

Exhibit 59

Reviews of *Glimpses of Bengal* (translation of *Chinnapatra by Surendranth Tagore)* and *The Wreck* (Translation of Noukadubi)—came out in *The Queen* (May 21, 1921).

Exhibit 60

Report on Tagore's tour in Vienna—*The Observer* (June 26, 1921).

Exhibit 61

Report on Tagore's play *The Farewell Curse* (Bidav Abhishap) staged at Hampstead—*The Morning Post* (September 5, 1921).

Exhibit 62

Report on Mahatma Gandhi's meeting *with* Tagore *at* Calcutta—*The Times* (September 12, 1921).

Exhibit 63

Report on *Tagore's play Trial by Luck* (Lakshmir Pariksha) staged by Union of East and West—*The Daily Chronicle* (October 24, 1921).

Exhibit 64

The Fugitive—selected translations of poems from *Kahini*—published by Macmillan in 1921. Reviews came out in *The Christian World* (November 17, 1921), *The Saturday Review* (November 19, 1921) and *The Sunday Times* (December 4, 1921).

Exhibit 65

The second biographical study *Rabindranath Tagore* by Edward Thompson was published by Macmillan in 1921. Review of the book appeared in *The New Statesman* (January 14, 1922).

Exhibit 66

Creative Unity—a collection of lectures delivered in USA during his tour in 1920-1921 was published in 1922. The two reviews exhibited came out in *The Saturday Review* (April 1, 1922) and in *The Literary Supplement* (May 25, 1922).

Exhibit 67

An article by G. Lower Dickinson on his personal impression of Tagore published in *The New Leader* (February 23. 1913).

Exhibit 68

The English translation of *Gora* by William Pearson was published by Macmillan in 1924. The reviews displayed were published in *The Nation* and *The Athenaeum* (February 9, 1924) and *The New Leader* (February 15, 1924).

Exhibit 69

A full page photograph of Tagore's play staged in Hampstead published in *The Graphic* (August 2, 1924).

Exhibit 70

Red Oleanders—translation of the play *Rakta Karabi* by the poet-was published by Macmillan in 1925. Two reviews of the drama were published in *The Times Literary Supplement* (July 9, 1925) and *Dublin Evening Mail* (July 22, 1925).

Exhibit 71

Red Oldeanders was not well received by the press. Eventually, Tagore had to explain the significance of the drama to his British readers through the media. An editorial on *Red Oleanders* and also the author's interpretation were published in the same issue of *The Manchester Guardian* (August 28, 1925).

Exhibit 72

A review of Broken Ties and Other Stories (a collection of short stories—published in 1925) appeared in *The Manchester Guardian* (November 20, 1925) and *The Times Literary Supplement* (January 14, 1926).

Exhibit 73

News of Tagore's visit to Italy—*The Daily News* (June 11, 1926).

Exhibit 74

Tagore's visit to Mussolini's fascist Italy (in 1926) was viewed obliquely by the rest of the non-fascist western press. During his stay in Italy Tagore did not realise the implications of his visit. At the end of the tour he joined Romain Rolland at his residence in Villeneuve. After discussion with Rolland he realised the evil of fascism. The above letter written to C.F. Andres *"On the philosophy of fascism"* was published in *The Manchester Guardian* (August 5, 1926).

Exhibit 75

"Tagore on fascims"—an editorial published in *The Manchester Guardian* (August 8, 1926).

Exhibit 76

In response to Tagore's letter published on August 5, Prof. Formici wrote a letter to the editor of *The Manchester Guardian* on Tagore's visit to Italy. This letter and an editorial came out in *The Manchester Guardian* on August 25, 1926.

Exhibit 77

"*Dr. Tagore on Fascism*"—a letter from Tagore to the editor of *The Manchester Guardian* (September 20, 1926).

Exhibit 78

A photograph of Tagore on his arrival in London in summer of 1926 was published in *Daily Graphic* on August 5.

Exhibit 79

"An Indian who conquered Europe"—an article by

S.K. Ratcliffe on the amazing vogue of Tagore in the Westwas published in *The Daily News* (August 7, 1926).

Exhibit 80

"A spot of verse"—a parody of Tagore's poem published in *The Daily Express* (August 7, 1926).

Exhibit 81

An interview of Tagore published in *The Westminster Gazette* (August 21, 1926).

Exhibit 82

Photographs of Tagore and his sculptor Jacob Epstein and Epstein's finished sculpture were published in *The Manchester Guardian* (October *12, 1926).*

Exhibit 83

An interview of H.N. Brailsford with Tagore was published in *The New Leader* (August 27, 1926). Sketch drawn by William Rothenstein.

Exhibit 84

Tagore's condemnation of Indian Nationalism—*The Times* (November 29, 1928).

Exhibit 85

Report on Allahabad Court case on copyright infringement (February 6, 1929) and the judgement (June 3, 1929) were publsihed in *The Times.*

Exhibit 86

News of Tagore's film—*The Times* (December 30, 1929).

Exhibit 87

A brief report on the Hibbert lectures on '*The Religion of Man*'—*The Times* (may 20, 1930).

Exhibit 88

A brief discussion on the work of Tagore published in *Oxford Mail* (May 27, 1930).

Exhibit 89

Tagore's paintings were exhibited in London on June *4, 1930* at British Indian Union Gallery. A brief report of this exhibition was published in *The Times* (June 5, 1930).

Exhibit 90

An article of Tagore published in *The Spectator* (June 7, 1930).

Exhibit 91

Tagore's interview in the Russian newspaper *Izvestia* was published in *The Manchester Guardian* (October 14, 1930).

Exhibit 92

A letter to the editor in *The Times* (May 16, 1932).

Exhibit 93

Tagore's appeal to the Prime Minister Baldwin to release political prisoners—*The Time*s (June 10, *1933).*

Exhibit 94

On Mahatma Gandhi's comment on Bihar earthquake—*The Times* (February 8, 1934).

Exhibit 95

Debate in the House of Commons on Tagore's article

published in *'Modern Review'—The Tinges* (November 13, 1934).

Exhibit 96

From 'Open Letters' series of correspondence between Prof. Gilbert Murrary and Tagore on the realisation of East and the *West-The Times* (February 6, 1935).

Exhibit 97

Ranald Newson—a poet and musician from Croydon, Surrey, joined Shantiniketan in 1935 as a visiting lecturer in English. When he left Shantiniketan Tagore gave him two of his paintings to be displayed at the Croydon Town Hall. This report was published in *The Times* (January 4, 1936). Photographs of those two paintings and a calligraphic note are exhibited in the adjoining panel.

Exhibit 98

An article on Indian literature published in *The Times Literary Supplement* (February 1, 1936).

Exhibit 99

An article on Tagore by E.J. Thompson published in *The Times* (February 23, 1940).

Exhibit 100

Tagore's appeal to US President to seek a solution to avert the War published in *The Times* (June 17, 1940).

Exhibit 101

News of Oxford honour to Tagore was published in several dailies. The exhibited report was published in The News Chronicle (August 8, 1940).

Rabindranath Tagore & The British Press, 1993 (Dr. Mulk Raj Anand inaugurating the Exhibition; The author on the extreme right)

Exhibit 102

An editorial on Oxford honour published in *The Times* (August 8, 1940).

Exhibit 103

Tagore's last message to the West—*The Manchester Guardian* (April 1, 1941).

Exhibit 104

News of death and obituary-*The Daily Telegraph* and *Morning Post* (August 8, 1941) and in *The Times* (August 8, 1941).

Exhibit 105

An obituary by E.J. Thompson published in *The Listener* on August 14, 1941.

On the occasion, 'Rabindranath and the British Press', a compilation of news reports and other items published in daily and weekly British newspaper during 1912 to 1941 published in book form by the Tagore Centre, London in 1990, was brought to the notice of the public. Prof. Mary M. Lago of University of Missouri, Columbia wrote in the Foreword to this volume that Tagore's appearance on the British literary scene in 1912 was an event of particular importance because a it inaugurated the first modern worldwide recognition of a living Indian writer. The responses of the British press are important because, in the historical context of British-Indian relations, they suggest reasons for his initial appeal and also for the decline in his popularity after the first World War... when a collection of his short stones was being prepared for an American publisher in 1965. those listed were previously untranslated stories in which Tagore wrote powerfully and sometimes bitterly about the problems of Bengali society. The publisher thought they were very fine but asked the translators to please include also "the sort of thing people expect from Tagore" that is, something gentler, more mystical, other wordily."

British Press knew little or nothing about his association early in the century with the protest against Lord Curzon's attempt to partition Bengal. Mary Lago further observes : As the press comments reveal, the decline in Tagore's populority in the West began when he applied his standards of humanist and political integrity to the world at large. When western critics and readers, carried away by the stale stereotype of the "spiritual East", had accused themselves of materialism, they had felt virtuously objective in selfcriticism. But when Tagore said the samething in statements that hit sharply home such as those in *Nationalism,* many in the West were outraged. Their gentle poet, their Wise Man from the East, had rejected their stereotype of him. It was inevitable that when he resigned his knighthood in 1919, in his own lonely and courageous protest against the Amritsar Massacre, the historical movement in Britain supporting General Dyer obscured the dignity of Tagore's gesture. It is worth noting that the selection of his short stories their being prepared for publication in English was severely restricted as Macmillan feared to publish the most outspoken of them because of the risk of being charged with sedition under British laws then in force."

7

TAGORE TRANSLATORS : AKADEMI LAUREATES

To encourage and to secure an all India recognition to writers writing in various Indian vernaculars, the Sahitya Akademi decided to give award every year since 1983 for the best work (may be a creative or a critical work) in the languages. Besides the Annual Awards for creative excellence, the Sahitya Akademi has also instituted *an Annual* Prize for *Translation from 1989* to be given to outstanding translations in the 22 languages recognized by it. Here the standing of the original writer and the excellence of the same work is taken into consideration and it ought to be a full, unabridged and faithful translation of the original work. While translation through a link language is also considered, preference is, however, given to a work of translation from the original language.

So far only four writers have bagged this awards for their translations of Tagore's writings. They are Sri B. Gopala Reddi (Telugu), Amar Bharati (Punjabi), Ramanlal P. Soni (Gujarati) and Surendra Jha 'Suman' (Maithili).

An acclaimed Telugu writer, translator, parliamentarian, Sri Bezawada Gopala Reddi was born on 5 August 1907 at Buchhireddipalem, a suburb town in Nellore district, Andhra Pradesh. He belonged to a family of erudite scholars, his father was a well known figure of his time, a great patron of poets who also founded a literary magazine in Telugu entitled 'Vartamana Tarangini' under the able editorship of his uncle Balakrishna Reddi.

Gopala Reddi had his primary education at Buchhireddi palem and Nellore. He pursed his further education from Andhra Jatiya Kalasala where he studied for about three and a half years. From there he moved to Shantiniketan to study at Visva-Bharati Universally of Rabindranath Tagore and stayed from 1924 to 1927. He was later awarded D.Litt. (honoris causa).

Author of twenty poetical works in Telugu, Gopala Reddi was a brilliant translator who was well conversant with Sanskrit, Bengali, Hindi and Urdu. He is accredited with invaluable rendering of Rabindranath Tagore, Ghalib and Iqbal. Some of his notable works are Visarjana, 1943; Chitrangada, 1945, Aru Natikalu (all plays); Urvasi, 1953, Kalidasu, 1954 (both poems), Malini, 1954; Prakriti Pratikaramu, *1954* (both plays) (All from Tagore).

First recipient of the Sahitya Akademi Award for Translation in Telugu in the year 1990, the work was also picked up for the Rajya Lakshmi Award (Madras, 1989) and K.V. Rao and Jyothi Rao Award (New York, 1989). An exmember of Sahitya Akademi and President of Andhra Pradesh Sahitya Akademi, Bezawada Gopala Reddi was the Chief Minister of Andhra Pradesh from 1955-56. He was elected to the Rajya Sabha for the term 1958-1961. He was elected to the Lok Sabha in 1962. Gopala Reddi served in the Union Government as the Minister of State for Revenue and Expenditure (1958-61), Minister of State for Works, Housing and Supply with independent charge (1961-62), Cabinet Minister for Information and Broadcasting (1962-63). He resigned from the Union Government *in 1963* under the 'Kamraj Plan' alongwith Morarji Desai, Lal Bahadur Shastri and others.

He became the Deputy Leader of the Congress Parliamentary Party in 1965 and served this 1967. From 1967 to 1972, he was the Governer of Uttar-Pradesh.

Sri Ramanlal P. Soni

(Winner of Sahitya Akademi Translation Prize, 1991 for his Gujrati version of Tagore's stories)

Prize in Punjabi to Amar Bharti (b. 1926) for his translation of Tagore's Short stories : Ikki Kahaniyan.

Award in Maithili to Surendra Jha 'Suman' (b. 1910) for his translation from Bengali of Rabindranath Tagore's Three Plays : Chirakumar Sabha, Visarjan and Chitrangada

Winner of *'Desh Puraskar'* from the Nikhil Bharat Banga Sahitya Sammelan, and *'The Sahitya Sameeksha Board Award* (Punjab), Sri Amar Bharti is a well known Punjabi author and critic who was born in Lopoke village in Lyalpur district (now in Pakistan). He was the Chief Editor of the Punjabi daily *Nawan Hindustan* for six years and of *Abheet* for a year. Besides a number of original works to his credit he has published more than ten volumes of translations from the Bengali classics and one volume of Tolstoy.

'Ikki Kahaniyan' is his translation of twenty one Bengali short stories by Tagore into Punjabi. The warm compassion of the original, its concern for the oppressed and the downtrodden, and its sensitive understanding of the plight of women, are effectively rendered in this book which won the prize for Punjabi for the year 1990. His translation succeeds admirably in capturing both the rootedness of the original in its native culture and its appeal that transcends the local.

A social worker and author of children literature in Gujarati, Sri Ramanlal P. Soni was born in 1908 at Kakapur village in Sabarkantha district of Gujarat. He was a Member of the Bombay Legilative Assembly for five years. Sri Ramanlal has to his credit several volumes of poetry, nursery rhymes and plays for children. He has translated copiously from Tagore, Saratchandra Chatterji. Among the various awards he has received are the NCERT and Govt. of Gujarat awards for children literature *Kabuliwala* contains thirty-seven stories in translation of Tagore's famous collections of short stories, *Galpaguchchha*. This book which bagged Translation Prize for the year 1991 in Gujarati is widely acclaimed for its felicity in recreating the moods and subtleties of Tagore's fiction, the work reads remarkably like an original. For its perceptive and masterly transference of the richness and diversity of the original into Gujarati, this work is regarded as a significant addition to Indian literature in Gujarati translation.

Surendra Jha 'Suman' was born in 1910 in Ballipur, Bihar. A renowned poet and author in Maithili, Sri Jha obtained his 'Kavyatirth' from the Sanskrit College, Calcutta and 'Shiksha-Sahityacharya' from Muzaffarpur Sanskrit College, Bihar, topping in both the examinations. An eminent journalist and academic, Sri Surendra Jha taught Maithili in Mithila University for nearly three decades and had been the Head of the Maithili Department, Bihar University. He also served as a member by Bihar Legislative Assembly and Later as a members of Lok Sabha.

He authored over 50 books of poetry, criticism and translation in Maithili, Sanskrit and Hindi. He edited a number of journals including Mithila-Mihar (193552) and Vaidehi (1949-64), a monthly in Maithili to name a few.

Several literary institutions have felicitated him for his contribution to literature and the honours and awards he has received include Sahitya Akademi Award and Vidyapati Puraskar. In 1971, for his poetry collection 'Payasvini', he was conferred the Sahitya Akademi Award in Maithili. It contains 25 lyrics depicting the beauty of nature and simplicity of rural life. For its colourful imagery and metrical experimentation, the work has been regards as a significant contributions to the contemporary Maithili Literature.

'*Rabindra Natakavali* Vol. 1' which received the Sahitya Akademi Translation Prize in Maithili language is an outstanding translation of the three plays of Rabindranath *Chirakumar Subha, Visarjan* and *Chitrangada.* For its exhilarating rendering, of the original, its innovative style, its sensitivity to language and the sheer authenticity of its portrayal of human life, Rabindra Natakavali is a significant contribution to Indian drama in translation.

8
TAGORE PUBLICATIONS

Sahitya Akademi is basically and primarily an association of Indian writers for promoting and coordinating literary activities in Indian languages. The exigencies of it programme have obliged the Akademi in the national interest to undertake the publication and distribution of books not normally published by private publishers.

Inspite of the pan Indian character of our literature, writers and readers in one language, know very little of what is being written in the neighbouring linguistic area. So, the Akademi has devised methods by which Indian. writers may come to known each other, cross the barriers of language and script, and appreciate the immense variety and complexity of their country's literary heritage. To a large extent, the Akademi seeks to meet this need through its publication programmes, such as bringing out bibliographies, histories of literatures, encyclopaedias, monographs, biographical reference sources, and also through its translation projects so that the great literary pieces emanating from the indigenous literatures and foreign works may be made available to the readers in their own language and not merely to the Englishknowing minority.

Sahitya Akademi has so far published over 3,000 books and it *is* bringing out one book every thirty two hours. Currently *it* has published over 150 books on and by Tagore in 22 languages is a great accomplishment.

It has published anothologies of Tagore poetry, short

stories, novels, plays, critical essays and also his biographies meant for both children and adult readers in all the major languages in India right from Assamese, Dogri, Gujarati, Hindi, Konkani, Maithili; Nepali, Urdu to Malayalam, Tamil and Telugu.

The popularity of Rabindranath can be gauged from the fact that writings of no other Indian author have been so widely translated as Tagore's.

From the very Centenary year of Rabindranath, Akademi is painstakingly engaged in bringing out Tagore writings in different vernaculars and has accepted books that give an authentic fresh and critical insights into his life and works.

Co-operation with UNESCO

From the very beginning, the Sahitya Akademi has actively co-operated with UNESCO, Paris, in the implementation of UNESCO's major project of Mutual Appreciation of Eastern and Western Cultural Values, and has also maintained contact with several literary and cultural institutions in foreign countries to encourage better appreciation of Indian literature abroad. Besides advising on matters of common interest, the Akademi has prepared for UNESCO many a publications.

UNESCO has also sponsored publication of translation of Indian classics in consultation with the Sahitya Akademi. Special mention could be made here of English renderation of select writings of Tagore entitled 'A *Tagore Reader'*, and in French, *Balaka* (poems), Gora (novel) and *Bhikharini and other .stories,* all the three by Rabindranath Tagore.

Binodini

'Binodini' the English version of Tagore's original

novel 'Chokher Bali' (lit. Eyesore) was first published in 1902. This is the first modern novel in Bengali where Tagore is at its best as storyteller. It is said that of all women characters created by Tagore in his many novels, Biodini is the most real, convincing and fullblooded.

Binodini is also the first most significant work by which Tagore established himself as a novelist of high order. Again probably, the first psychological novel of India. Its action revolves around the mental conflicts of its all characters, dealing with the dilemma of human relationship.

Its English rendering done by Krishna Kripalani was first published by the Akademi in 1959. A revised edition in 1968. The third, fourth and fifth editions came out in 1977, 1982 and 1991 respectively. The translator clarify that the liberty in changing the title of the book may be excused it is recalled that in the first synopsis of the story jotted down by the author in his note-book the title originally conceived and given by him was 'Binodini'.

Chaturanga

Originally published serially in the journal *Sabujpatra* in 1915, this novel of Tagore appeared in book form in 1916, published by Indian Press, Allahabad.

This is an extremely powerful novel of Tagore where he used the four parts—exposition, development, variation and recapitulataion. He was deeply attached to this form, its varying rhythms and speeds and this underlying musical form gives the book its textures, its many voices and its symbolic quality.

An important English translation by this novel is by Asok Mitra. The book was published by the Akademi in 1963. A reprint came out in 1996.

The English Writings of Rabindranath Tagore

To mark the 50th death anniversary of Gurudev Rabindranath Tagore, the three National Akademies in collaboration with ICCR organised an International Seminar on '*Tagore's Vision of India-: Its Relevance Today*' from 7 to 9 August 1991 at New Delhi. In his address of welcome, the Secretary, Sahitya Akademi announced that the Akademi would soon bringout in three volumes, the complete writings of Tagore in English and in English translation. Eventually Volume I was published in 1994 and reprinted in 1997. Volumes II and III were broughtout in 1996.

The volumes contain his original as well as translations done by him. The corpus of his English writings, large and diverse, forms a substantial part of his total work. The first volume includes all the poetic works translated by Tagore and the poems that he wrote originally in English. The second volume consists of plays and stories translated by him, as well as five prose works. The third is a collection of differet genres of writings—six prose works including the Hibbert Lectures, The Religion of Man, a large number of lectures and addresses on various issues, public statements and messages, and conversations with some of the eminent persons of this century—Einstein, Croce, Rolland and Gandhi.

This monumental work is edited by Dr. Sisir Kumar Das who was Tagore Professor at the University of Delhi

Gora

Gora is the longest novel of epic proportion written by Tagore at the back drop of the most crucially intellectual era of modern history Akademi has translated this novel which is the fifth in order of his novel writing (1909) into English and many Indian languages.

In its publication process, some times some awkward situations do arises. D.S. Rao in his *'Three decades' : a short history of Sahitya Akademi, 1954-84* informs "As part of the Tagore Centenary Programme, the Oriya translation of Goru had been assigned to a translator on the recommendation of the Oriya Advisory Board. The translation in manuscript was read and approved by the convenor of the Board, and on his recommendation the translator was paid his remuneration and the manuscript was sent to press in Cuttuck. After the main text was printed and an advance copy was received, it was noticed that the numbers of pages in the Oriya, translation was considerably less than in the original Bengali edition. A check-up of the copy by a local Oriya scholar revealed that large portions of the original text were missing from the translation at several places. The Convener and the translator were requested to explain the serious omissions. The Convener stated that he had not checked the entire manuscript in detail and that his approval related only to the quality of the translation. He expressed regret that the translator had betrayed his trust. The translator, on the other hand, stated that he had abridged the work in translation to make it more readable for Oriya readers. The Oriya Advisory Board considered the matter and resolved that the present translation of Gora being incomplete, should be rejected and the translator "be called upon to submit a fresh, full and faithful translation of the novel without any additional remuneration and to com ensate the Sahitya Akademi for the losses incurred in printing the present translation." The Executive Board of the Akademi approved that the copies of the abridged Oriya edition already printed should be destroyed. The Convener resigned his position on the Oriya Advisory Board.

Of late, the English translation of this novel by Sujit

Mukheijee was broughtout by the Akademi in 1997. This translation represents the fuller text as it appears now in *Rabindracharachandabali* while an earlier version into English, often ascribed to Tagore's nephew Surendranath, was published in 1924 by Macmillan & Co of London (periodically reprinted). That text probably rendered the original as it appeared with some deletions in book form in 1909.

In Your Blossoming Flower Garden : Rabindranath Tagore and Victoria Ocampo

This fascinating book by Ketaki Kushari Dyson deals with the rare encounters of Tagore and Victoria Ocampo—young Argentine woman who was a devoted admirer of his works. There is a wealth of documentary evidence, including the presentation of valuable archival material, the entire known Tagore-Ocampo correspondence with full annotations and 33 black and white coloured plates, some of which have never been published before. The book appeared in print in 1988.

Kavi Katha

'Kavi Katha' short biographical sketch of Tagore for children written by Lilā Majumdar. This book originally written in Bengali has been rendered into various other Indian languages and broughtout by the Akademi from time to time. (Second edition published in 1967)

Modernism and Tagore

This book by Abu Syeed Ayyub which won Akademi Award in Bengali in the year 1970 and a year before, Rabindra Puraskar was published by the Sahitya Akademi in English in 1988 and translated by Amitava Ray. The book is a significant effort in evaluating Tagore's literary genius in the background of modernism which according to the author chiefly consists in a single minded preoccupation with the body of poetry with the consequent belief in the self sufficiency of language and in an oppressive and overwhelming consciousness of evil in the world.

Rabindranath Tagore

On the occasion of his 125th birth anniversary, a monograph on Tagore penned by Sisir Kumar Ghose, broughtout by the Akademi was released by the Prime Minister of India in 1986. This monograph was published under the series "Makers of Indian Literature".

According to Sisir Kumar Ghose, the monograph is not a Tagore primer or a 'guide' to Tagore's plenty. A sample survey, it but offers a bird's eye-view of a baffling, breathtaking creativity. A quick survey of his eventful life, the poetry, drama, novels, short stories is followed by his seminal thoughts on the Religion of Man (perhaps more of one man than of all men), the ideas in Art and Beauty, and a utopian plan for an Education for Fullness. There is a summing up at the end, a sort of salute rather than the last word. One can always make new discoveries. May the readers make their own."

Rabindrarachana Sanchayana

An anthology in Hindi translation of select writings of Rabindranath Tagore compiled by Asis Kumar Bandyopadhyay was released by the Vice-President of India in 1987.

***"Rabindranath Tagore, 1861-1961* : A Centenary Volume"**

This exhaustive book was broughour by the Akademi in 1961 with an introduction by *Pandit Jawaharlal Nehru and* interesting note by *Sarvepalli Radhakrishnan entitled*

'Most dear to all the muses'. Many eminent scholars and *creative people* contributed to this *volume. For interested* readers, the Table of Contents is given below

Personal Memories

Uncle *Rabindranath/Indira Devi Chaudhurani*

Personal Memories of *Tagore Leonard Elmhirst*

Tagore on the Banks of *the River Plate/Victoria Ocampo*

Father as I Knew Him/*Rabindranath Tagore*

Recollections of Tagore/*Giuseppe Tucci*

Studies and Appreciations

Tagore, Reconciler of East and West/*Mulk Raj Anand*

Tagore and Indian Culture/*Rukmini Devi Arundale*

The Aesthetic Philosophy of Tagore/*Abu Sayeed Ayyub*

Tagore and Western Music/Arnold *Adrian Bake*

Tagore as a Novelist/*Bhabani Bhattacharya*

Rabindranath Tagore and Bengali Prose/*Buddhadeva Bose*

Tagore's Relations with England/*Vera Brittain*

A World Poet/Pearl Buck

Visva-Manah *Vak-Pati/Suniti Kumar Chatterji*

The Universal Man/Richard Church

Rabindranath and Sanskrit Literature/*Atulchandra Gupta*

Tagore's Poetic Vision/*Umashankar Joshi*

Social and Political Ideas of Tagore/*Humayun Kabir*

A Homage to Tagore from Japan/*Toshihiko Katayania*

Rabindranath Tagore and My Father/*Arnold Keyserling*
Leos Janacek and Rabindranath Tagore/*Somnath Maitre*

Tagore as a Writer for Children/*Lila Majumdar*

Tagore's *Music/Dhurjati P*rasad Mukerji

Tagore and Jimenez : Poetic Coincidences/*Graciela Palau de Nemes*

Drawings and Paintings of Rabindranath Tagore/ *Prithwish Neogy*

Tagore and the Nobel Prize/*Anders Osterling*

Tagore, Poet of Mankind/*Alexandru Philippide*

Let's Commemorate Tagore with Unity and Friendship *Ping-Hsin*

Rabindranath, An Artist in Life/*Annada Sankar Ray*

Rabindranath Tagore and the Indian Tradition *Niharranjan Ray*

The Plays of Rabindranath Tagore/*Hirankumar Sanyal*

Tagore as Poet-Education/*Sunilchandra Sarkar*

Western Influence of the Poetry of Tagore/*Taraknath Sen*

Rabindranath's Short Stories *Nirmal Kumar Sidhanta*

The Real Rabindranath Tagore and His Music/*Philippe Stem*

'Tagore, The Goethe of India'/Albert *Schweitzer*

'Tagore's Poetry Overflowed National Boundaries/ *Robert Frost*

Tagore In Other Lands

Tagore, Great Son of the Indian People/ *Auezov. Chel yshev. Tikhonov. Tursun-Zade. Tychina*

Tagore's Visit to Saim/*Sonakul Dhani*

Tagore in Holland/*Ben van Eysselstein*

Tagore in the West/*Pierre Fallon S.J.*

Tagore and Germany/*Theodor Heuss*

Tagore in Bulgaria/*Vicho Ivanov*

Gitanjali in Iceland/*Halldor Laxness*

Tagore and Brazil/*Cecilia Meireles*

Tagore in Asia/*Kalidas Nag*

Tagore in Poland/*Tadeusz Pobozniak*

Tagore and Norway/*Egil Richard Rasmussen*

Tagore and *Vietnam/Nguyen-Dang-Thuc*

Tagore and Czechoslovakia/*Dusan Zbavitel*

Offerings

Some Ethical Concept for the Modern World from Hindu and Indian Buddhist Tradition/*W. Norman Brown*

The Implications of Indian Ethics for International Relations/*Amiva Chakravarty*

Early Sinological Studies at Santiniketan/*Vasudev Gokhale*

'The One In the Rig Veda/*Stella Kramrisch*

The Music of India/*Narayana Menon*

Indological Studies in India/*Venkatarama Raghavan*

Chronicle and Bibliography

Rabindranath Tagore : A Chronicle of Eighty Years. 1861-1941/Prabl2crtkumar Mukhopadhyaya, Kshitis Roy.

Works of Rabindranath Tagore : A Bibliography/ *Pulinbihari Seta, Jagadindra Bhaumik*

Sahitya Akademi is one of the biggest publisher of books in India and designs its publications in a such a way that it reflect the variety, the underlying unity of India's rich literature and the uniqueness. It's uniqueness can simply be judged from its invaluable transliterated volumes.

In this store house of books, one can find Tagore's Bengali works in Devanagari script also.

These are :—

1. Bal Sahitya/edited by *Lila Majumdar and Kshits Ray* and transliterated by *Yugajit,* Nawalpuri, 1962, Selection of Tagore's writing for Children.
2. Chokher Bali/transliterated by *Manorama Bajpai,* 1961.
3. Ekavimsati/transliterated by *Harishankar Sharma;* intod. by *Somnath Maitra,* (21 short stories of Tagore, 1963)
4. Ekottarasati/transliterated by *Ramapujan Tiwari,* foreward by *Humayun Kabir,* (101 poems of Tagore, 1958)
5. Gita Panchasati/transliterated by *Rampujan Tiwari;* ed. by *Indira Devi Chaudharani,* (50 select song of Tagore, 1960)
6. Gora/transliterated by *Konika Briswas,* 1961.
7. Natya Saptak Vol. 1/tranliterated by *Rampujan Tiwari;* introd. by *Pramathnath Bisi.* Includes *Bisarjan, Chitrangada* and *Chirakumar Sabha* (All plays, 1963)

8 Nibandhamala Vol. 1/transliterated by *Indranath*

Choudhari : introd. by Kazi Abdul Wadud. (select essays of Tagore, 1969)

9. Nibandhamala Vol. II/transliterated by *Dwijram Yadav;* introd. by *Buddhadeva Bose* (select essays of Tagore, 1970)
10. Yogayog, transliterated by *Konika Biswas,* 1963.

9

SAMVATSAR LECTURES

The Annual Festival of Letters the most spectacular literary event that is celebrated every year in winter, usually in the occasion month of February. The striking features of this event are the inauguration of the Akademi Exhibition, the Annual Samvatsar Lectures, the Annual Award Presentation Ceremony, the Writers Meet and lastly a Seminar with which the function concludes.

The Samvatsar Lectures are given by an established writer and a creative thinker who has profound understanding of Indian literature. These lectures were instituted in 1985 by resolution of the Executive Board dated 24 February 1985, that accepted the recommendations of the Committee set up for the establishment of a series of lectures in literary criticism. A procedure was described by the Board for the selection of the annual Samvatsar lectures. The Samvatsar lecture is expected to deliver two or three lectures on a theme chosen by him. It was also laid down that these Samvatsar lectures would be published after they are delivered. The crucial clauses in the resolution relating to the Samvatsar lectures read as follows :

These lectures should reflect a deep concern for values. They should open up a new vistas of thinking regarding a literary movement, a current literary trend, some original thinking about a great classic or a new path in literary criticism or literary creation, etc. The presentation should be from in larger perspective while the subject matter could be drawn from the regional or comparative sources within the speaker's experience. So far, many scholars have delivered Samvatsar Lectures, the first one being by Sri S.H. Vatsyayan "Agyena" on 12 March 1986.

However, I shall epitomize chiefly those lectures which have taken up for examination Tagore's creative works and thoughts and also select scholars who have made passing references to Rabindranath or his writings. a,7

The Second Samvatsar Lectures entitled "*In Retrospect*" were delivered by Annada Shankar Ray on 21-22" February 1987. He gave two lectures : the first titled *"The Sea Change"* and the second on *"The Elite and The People"*. In the two lectures on Bengali Renaissance written after forty years since the end of the British period, Sri Ray has prued his mind of all passion and reflected dispassionately over the past. Some of his observations made for the first, time may compel us to review our own ideas of the Renaissance for their freshness and vivacity. Armada Shankar observes that in Bengal the Renaissance includes the Reformation and the Enlightenment. A part from Ram Mohan and Vidyasagar the three towering figures of the Bengal Renaissance were Michael Madhusudan Datta, Bankim Chandra Chatterjee and Rabindranath Tagore. He adds that Hindu Revivalism felt that though the spiritual East had nothing to learn from the materialist West, Science was an exception. In return, the West should learn spirituality from the East. An honourable relationship was only possible on a basis of give and take. India was to give spirituality and take science. Europe should give science and take spirituality Swami Vivekananda sailed for America with India'; spiritual gift to the West. He returned with disciplines from there. Sister Nivedita was the Hindu name of one of his Western disciplines. She became an Indian by adoption.

But could she be a Hindu without being born into a Hindu caste, such as Brahmin or Kayasth a on Vaidya in Bengal?

This was a veryinteresting question and it probably induced Rabindranath to write his monumental novel, Gora, observed Armada Shankar Ray. In his words :—

Gora is the son of an Irish couple who lost their lives during the Sepoy Mutiny. He was picked up and adopted by a childless Brahmin couple in Northern India. He grows up in the belief that he is a born Brahmin, lineal descendant of Vedic Rishis. His great aspiration is to revive the wonder that was Ancient India; it would be so much better than the present reality. He hates the British and dislikes the Brahmos. Yet he is in love with a Brahmo girl, Sucharita. His adoptive mother is free from caste and communal prejudice, but her husband is not. Suddenly taken ill and apprehending death the husband is more aware of what could happen to him in the other world, if a *mlechchha* performs his funeral rites. So he discloses to Gora his real identity. Gora falls from the skies. He has no one to call his own. All the temples of India are closed to him. At this crisis Sucharita assures him of her love and her foster father approves their engagement. Anandamayi, his adoptive mother, tells him that he is her only child and she will die if he leaves her. Fortunately Krishnadayal, his adoptive father, survives. So there is no immediate break in the family. Gora bows to Anandamayi saying, "Mother, t you are my India. You have no caste and no religion. You are simply an embodiment of welfare."

Tagore found no place for Gora in Hindu society. but in the Brahmo Samaj. This too was not his father', but Keshab Chandra's Samaj where such a marriage was permissible. But what he wanted to drive home was that India is greater than Hindu and an Irish child can be an

Indian by naturalisation without being a Hindu by birth. His vision of India was all-inclusive. In his famous poem beginning with "*He mor chitta*" he elaborated the idea : "O my heart, slowly awaken on the shore of this sea of great humanity, this sacred land, this India. Here mingled the Aryans, the Non-Aryans, the Sakas, the Hunas, the Pathans, the Mughals. No one went away. They merged in one Being. They all live in me." He proceeds to welcome the English into the harmony that is India. They too have something to offer for her fulfilment.

The song that has become our National Anthem *Janaganamana* was composed in the same strain, with the same vision before his inner eyes. His concept of India was allinclusive. Unity amidst diversity was the motif of the song."

Armada Shankar Ray, however, regrets that the Muslim psyche was afraid of Tagore's concept of India as the 'sea of great humanity' where all the separate streams merge themselves and become one. To the Muslim mind India was Hindustan, the land of the Hindus, where merger meant Hinduisation. Indianisation was an unknown idea. In any case, Indianisation of the posts held by the Europeans virtually meant Hinduisation as the Muslims could not compete. Surely Muslims had not come all the way from Arabia, Iran, central Asia and Afghanistan to be lost in the land of isolators. It they could not go back to their old homelands they could carve out a new homeland where they could escape merger.

The seventh lecture in the series was delivered by professor All Ahmed Suroor, an outstanding Urdu critic and scholar. It was entitled '*Literature : the question and the answer?* The lecture was in two parts. In the first lecture '*Has Literature Failed*'. Professor Suroor argues that great literature never fails; but literature which is impelled by considerations of fashion and affirmations of endless meanderings into the unconscious has indeed failed.

He feels that there are no great names in the Indian literary scene like those of Tagore and Iqbal and Premchand. The age of giants is over. He further insists that to appreciate the immense variety and complexity of our own literary heritage and to meet the challenge posed by multilingual society, we need more and more translations from one Indian language to another, and many from world languages. Who *can deny the influence of Bankimchandra Chatterjee, Tagore on Hindi and other Indian languages,* on the impact of Meer and Ghalib apart from that of some outstanding Urdu short story writers, or the influence of Goethe, Tolstoy, Chekhov, Dostoevsky, Eliot, W.B. Yeats, Thomas Mann, Moliere, Sartre, Camus, Kafka, Brecht and Becket on Indian literature, or even the influence of oriental literature on Goethe, Coleridge, Arnold and others. It is a fact of history."

Samvatsar Lecture-IX was delivered by Prof. Navakanta Barua on 16th & 17th February 1994. He spoke on "*Folkways in Literature : An Aesthetic Imperative.*" Sri Barua believes that olkreality is an infinitely self-sustaining area. As a poet he had initiated that exploration of folkways which helped evolve the idiom of modern Assamese poetry. His novels and analytical writings reveal a profound sense of history and tradition, a thorough going modern sensibility and a comprehensive range of concerns and, finally he close in on Goethe who had deliberately exploited folkways and idioms to afford us a view of his complex modern vision.

Dr. Barua points out that *like Sankaradeva,* the early *Rabindranath Tagore, the seer-poet of modern India, did not accommodate folk cults and ways in his envisioned synthesis of the Upanishads, Buddhism and Western humanism.* After giving a brief reference to the range and the divergence of the exploration of folkways in literature, with illustrations mostly from the European continent. Dr. Barua tried to explain how it became an aesthetic imperative for a fifteenth century Assamese poet and preacher, Sankardeva, who was a staunch advocate of the 'chaste' literary style kept free from vulgar, folk elements widening our fos, we train our sight on Tagore's *near ambivalent attitude towards the popular and folk practices of his time, sub-conscious, images and metaphor immersed in folk cults and practices like the mother-goddess and others.* Infact for the context of feelings, from which the later poems emerge we have to look beyond to an older, more earthy and rather esoteric occultism. The Bauls and the Vaishnavas could be rationally accomodated but the Tantric world, first accorded recognition as devices, later on poured forth from the innermost depths of his psyche and his deep-seated realism did not resist His faith, after all, was sufficiently strong to face the facts. To quote Navakanta Barua "*Rabindranath, in his formative period (his whole creative career being ever formative though)* would not yield to the great prevalence of the mother cult and the sub-terrenian occult Tantricism. He was aware of their vital presence, but they were never significant in the formation of his poetic personality. The early Tagore knew of the dacoit communities of Southern Bengal around Calcutta, all worshipper of Kali. In *Valmiki Prabbha they make their appearance singing Ramprasadi strains with Western operatic modes. But Rabindranath was on the side of the mildly musical Veenapani and against the ferocious Mother Kali. In. Bisarjan, too, he was out and out opposed to animal sacrifice to the goddess. Tantricism* and the mother goddesses were not his cup of Okakura Tea. He was aesthetically averse to such earthy ethics.

In *Chandalika*, a much later work, Tantric machinery crept in rather stealthily; as if from the sub terrenian depths of the unconscious. We find *Dakinis* (like Goethe's Phorkides) being invoked to bring back the phantom Ananda Even though it is a device, if represents something alien to Tagore's psychological stance, and in his latter poems right from *Prantik* down to *Shesh Lekha,* we find glimpses of intimate tantric imagery, as I have already indicated, enriching his word music to the status of *mantras.* It can be looked at as an uttervescence of pristine tantrism on an upanishadic and Buddhist awareness of reality..."

Noted Hindi writer, Nirmal Verma in his Samvatsar Lectures-XI in two parts on concept of '*Truth in Art*' states that Man on earth is a fragile creature-incomplete, weak and vulnerable but in a work of art, in a painting or in a piece of music or in a poem, he is able to get a fleeting glimpse of what can be called the 'advaitic' feeling of wholeness from which he has been exiled by the forces of history and the fragmentary nature of life. To Verma, a work of art does not communicate truth—it is the truth itself. It carries within itself multiple layers of meaning, coexisting or sometimes colliding. A work of art acquires the numinous quality of the sacred—a 'return' to the primal sense of our being. He strongly believes that the truth in art can never be governed by the evolutionary laws of progress. The progress in art is an illusion.

In this lecture, Nirmal Verma points out that Tagore gives us a clue to the essence of truth in art it, does not change the world nor does it pretend to change us-what it does is more fundamental, more profound—it changes the nature of our relationship with the world and in the process changes both us and the world. Verma picks up Tagore's novel 'Gora' to justify it. Gora, the central character finds his true identity precisely in an epiphanic moment of self-discovery. Stripped off all his selfimposed social masks, of being an orthodox Hindu or patriotic Bengali, a saviour of Bharat Mata, he goes beyond himself, back to his own self-hood: Or shall we say to his saint hood? To quote Verma again, "Tagore, it is said had Vivekananda in his mind as prototype which he wanted to recreate in Gora. And yet what he created in his novel was just the opposite—Vivekananda renounced the world to reach out to realize his true self, while Gora abandoned his asceticism to enter the world with a new insight about himself. His 'saintliness' if we may use such a term for Gora, arises not from faith, but from doubt, when the starts questioning the worth of all the baggage he was carrying on his back—the baggage of false identities. By shedding them he becomes free. This freedom he earned not by renouncing the world but by establishing a new relation with the reality which was a part of his self and of which he was oblivious... In this miraculous act of metamorphosis, Tagore, seemed to be following not the model of Vivekananda, which in any case was nothing more than superficial device of resemblance, but his Guru, Swami Ramkrishna Paramashansa."

Subhas Mukhopadhyay who with his intense identification with the suffering, became a true 'people's poet' in his Samvatsar Lectures-XII entitled *'Tagore without Bounds' take up for examination Rabindranath Tagore's poetry. and thought.* Lit up by his ersonal reminiscences of Tagore's impact on him as the was growing up in the 1920s in a small town in Bengal, the address highlights Tagore's relevance today in India in particular and the world in general. Tagore today is not confined to his readers alone. Those who cannot read him, approach Tagore through their ears. There was a time when the elite of Bengal fought among themselves to monopolise Tagore. They tried to seal off Tagore, cordoning him away from the hoi polloi. There was another trend, serving the same purpose, but in a different way. In the name of ideology and as the sole representative of the masses, some tried to protect the proletariat from the bourgeois poet's harmful influence! Mukhopadhyay quotes from Tagore's verses which they quoted and misinterpreted his words such as one "... *Sammāner chiranirbasane Samajer uchcha manche basecchi sangkeerna bātāyane Amar kabita, jani ami ...*".... (Exiled or life to the realm of veneration, I sit on the narrow portico of society's high pulpit. Occasionally I ventured near the courtyard on the other side, but as my courage failed me, I could not get in ... I know, although my poetry has covered diverse paths, it could not reach every where). Subhas Mukhopadhyay further writes : It is ridiculous to draw from this the conclusion, as they did, that Tagore himself attributed this limitations to his bourgeois class origins! Actually the context here is quite different. As Tagore says at the beginning of the same poem : *Bipulā e prithibeer Katotuku Jāni,* (How little do I know of this vast world?). He then continues.

"Ami prithibur kobi

Jethā tar jato uthe dhvani" .... *Antar mīshāle tabe tar antarer parichay*

(I am a poet of the universe. My flute wakes up to respond to every vibration from any corner of that universe. But in spite of my unrelentingly worshipful effort to capture them, many a sound failed to reach me. There are gaps... Man, in his innermost self, is the most inaccessible; one cannot measure him in terms of time and space. He lives in his own self. Only by mingling one's heart with his, can one get to know his inner self. I cannot find every where the do or to enter that self. The stumbling blocks are the enclosures that surround my lifestyle.

Tagore expresses here his sense of sadness at not being able to be omnipresent and omniscient. Given this context, it was sheer tomfoolery to hunt for a class angle in a poet's intense derive to become one with the whole."

Mukhopadhyay picks up his favourite stanzas from Tagore to explain the poet's concept of life and death, beginning and end, old and new. Starting from the earlier poems composed by Tagore at the and of the 19th century he takes us through the poet's long journey to his last poems written on his deathbed-Subhas Mukhopadhyay also takes up Tagore's prose writings and examines his response towards a variety of contemporary themes like modernism in literature, nationalism in politics, restructuring of the Indian economy, upliftment of the poor, the Second World War and its destructive impact. What emerges is the picture of the complete man-the poet and visionary who refused to be a recluse and was ever alert and ready to respond to the needs of his country.

All there lectures have been broughtout by the Akademi in book form.